HENRIK IBSEN'S
HEDDA GABLER

IN A NEW VERSION BY
BRIAN FRIEL

DRAMATISTS
PLAY SERVICE
INC.

SPECIAL NOTE

HEDDA GABLER received its world premiere at The Gate Theatre, in Dublin, Ireland, on September 30, 2008. It was directed by Anna Mackmin; the set design was by Lez Brotherston; the lighting design was by Oliver Fenwick; and the original music was by Denis Clohessy. The cast was as follows:

HEDDA GABLER .... Justine Mitchell
GEORGE TESMAN .... Peter Hanly
JULIANA TESMAN .... Susan FitzGerald
BERTHA .... Billie Traynor
EILERT LOEVBORG .... John Light
THEA ELVSTED .... Andrea Irvine
JUDGE BRACK .... Andrew Woodall

CHARACTERS

HEDDA GABLER — 29, daughter of General Gabler and wife of George

GEORGE TESMAN — 33, research graduate in cultural history.

JULIANA TESMAN — 65, George's aunt

BERTHA — 60, Juliana's maid

EILERT LOEVBORG — 33, writer and sociologist

THEA ELVSTED — 26, wife of a resident magistrate

JUDGE BRACK — 45

PLACE

The Tesman house in a fashionable part of the city.

TIME

The year 1890.

Act One
An early morning in September.

Act Two
That afternoon.

Act Three
Dawn the following day.

Act Four
That evening.

SET

A large drawing room decorated in dark colours and carefully furnished — a round table, chairs, an armchair, a footstool, a porcelain stove, an upright piano.

In the left-hand wall (left and right from the point of view of the audience), a door leads to the hall. In the right-hand wall, a French window with the curtains pulled back. Through this window we see part of a verandah and autumn trees.

In the back wall of the drawing room, a wide doorway with its curtains pulled back. Through it we see a smaller room with decor and furnishings similar to the drawing room — round table, sofa, chairs, terra-cotta ornaments. Clearly visible on a wall in this smaller room is a large portrait of an elderly General Gabler, Hedda's father, resplendent and formidable in full military uniform.

There are several bunches of fresh flowers on the drawing room table, on top of the piano and in vases around both rooms.

HEDDA GABLER

ACT ONE

Juliana Tesman comes in from the hall. She is a pleasant, kindly spinster in her mid-sixties. She is in outdoor clothes, wearing a hat, carrying a parasol. She pauses and looks round the silent drawing room.

JULIANA. *(Softly to herself.)* I was afraid of that.

BERTHA. *(Offstage.)* What's that, Miss?

JULIANA. Shhhh! *(Bertha enters. She is a few years younger than Juliana. She is carrying a bunch of flowers.)*

BERTHA. What did you say, Miss Juliana?

JULIANA. Keep your voice down, Bertha. We're too early. They're not up yet.

BERTHA. He must be exhausted.

JULIANA. They both must be exhausted.

BERTHA. Why wouldn't he be? It was all hours before the steamer berthed. And then, when she got up here, nothing would do her but she'd unpack everything *before* she went to bed.

JULIANA. She's a very efficient young woman.

BERTHA. Why does she call me Berna then?

JULIANA. She just misheard your name.

BERTHA. Huh! She must have had a dozen trunks of stuff.

JULIANA. Four, Bertha; just four.

BERTHA. And nine boxes — I counted them.

JULIANA. *(Ironically.)* Good for you. *(Juliana throws open the French windows.)* Well, let them have a good lie-in. And put those flowers down somewhere.

BERTHA. Where?

JULIANA. There — anywhere. And when they do come down

they can fill their lungs with good Norwegian air.

BERTHA. Where will I put — ?

JULIANA. Give them to me. (*Juliana takes the flowers brusquely out of Bertha's hand and puts them on top of the piano.*)

BERTHA. I'm never going to get the hang of this house, Miss Juliana.

JULIANA. Don't be silly.

BERTHA. (*Close to tears.*) It's not going to work out. I know it's not. And I'm afraid — (*Juliana puts her arms around her.*)

JULIANA. We'll have none of that, Bertha. You're going to be very happy here. Do you think I would have parted with you to anybody but Miss Hedda? And you'll have George, won't you? — our darling Georgie that you have taken care of since he was a baby. But what am I going to do without *you?*

BERTHA. You're the only family I've every known, you and Master George and lovely Miss Rena.

JULIANA. Very little will change. You'll just carry on looking after George in this house as you've always done all your life — and Mrs. George, too, of course. And I'll drop in as often as I can.

BERTHA. But that new maid you've got, she won't be able to look after Miss Rena. A big, rough lump like that, she wouldn't know how to handle an invalid.

JULIANA. She'll learn, Berna.

BERTHA. (*Cautioning.*) Miss!

JULIANA. Sorry. And I'll be there. We'll manage.

BERTHA. And Miss Hedda — Mrs. George — I just know she doesn't like me.

JULIANA. (*Wearily.*) "Doesn't like — " What nonsense is that! She scarcely knows you yet.

BERTHA. She's a cold woman.

JULIANA. And when you get to know each other you'll grow to love her — and not only because she's George's wife.

BERTHA. And a very bossy woman.

JULIANA. She's a determined young woman, yes. Isn't she the daughter of General Gabler? And brought up with a household of orderlies to boss around? Remember, we used to see her out riding with her father on an enormous black horse; in this elegant black riding dress?

BERTHA. And a feather in her hat, kind of defiant. Who would have thought that herself and our Georgie would ever have made a — ?

JULIANA. Not simply "our Georgie" anymore, Bertha. They made him a doctor when he was away in Germany. Our Georgie is now Doctor George Tesman.

BERTHA. I know.

JULIANA. And he is *so* thrilled by it: blurted it out last night before we were at the foot of the gangway. *(Realising.)* How did you know?

BERTHA. It was her first instruction when she stepped into this house. "From now on you'll address Mr. Tesman as Doctor Tesman."

JULIANA. Imagine if poor Joachim had lived to see his precious little boy grow into such an accomplished man. And there may be an even more important title coming his way soon.

BERTHA. Bigger than doctor?

JULIANA. Bigger than doctor.

BERTHA. What would be bigger than doctor?

JULIANA. Guess.

BERTHA. They're going to make a vet out of him!

JULIANA. He's not that kind of doctor, Bertha. He's an academic doctor. But when the other title comes along, as he would say himself, "My goodness. Oh my goodness." Anyhow … Why did you take the loose covers off the chairs?

BERTHA. She told me to — Miss Hedda. They remind her of shrouds, she said.

JULIANA. So they must be going to make this their living room then. *(George Tesman enters from the back room. He is thirty-three, genial, open, very enthusiastic. Judge Brack describes him as "decent, credulous, trusting" — in other words he can be simultaneously admirable and infuriating. He is carrying an empty suitcase.)* Good morning, George.

GEORGE. Auntie Juju! *(He embraces her excitedly.)* Well, isn't this a wonderful surprise first thing in the morning!

JULIANA. I'm afraid it *is* a bit early to —

GEORGE. Early? Not a bit! The earlier the better! And Bertha! *(He embraces her with equal enthusiasm.)* How are you, Bertha?

JULIANA. She hasn't slept for three nights waiting for you to come home.

BERTHA. It was the toothache really.

GEORGE. My very own Bertha! Look at the two of you! My goodness. Oh my goodness. I'm so glad to see you both. What a great joy to come down to this! And thank you for meeting us off the tender last night. That wasn't at all necessary.

JULIANA. I just dropped by to see that you're settled in.

GEORGE. As if we had lived here all our lives. We were so sorry we couldn't squeeze you into the carriage last night, Auntie Juju. But there was scarcely room for me with all darling Hedda's luggage.

BERTHA. A dozen trunks and nine boxes.

GEORGE. At least, Bertha! How did you get home?

JULIANA. Judge Brack saw me right up to my door.

GEORGE. Good for him. Well, what an unqualified joy to come down to this! As if I'd never left home! All we need now is lovely Auntie Rena and we'd be a complete family again. How is she?

JULIANA. I'm afraid my darling sister is slipping away slowly and very quietly.

GEORGE. Oh, Auntie Juju.

JULIANA. It's not easy to watch.

GEORGE. Must be awful.

JULIANA. I really think Bertha keeps her alive.

BERTHA. I wish I could.

GEORGE. I'm sure that's true.

JULIANA. You'll see a big change.

GEORGE. I'll go over today.

JULIANA. But if she weren't there — and now with you gone — my life would be hollow — wouldn't it?

GEORGE. I'm not gone, Auntie Juju! I'm very much here! *(She kisses his cheek.)* And I'll always be here!

BERTHA. Is there anything I can do for Miss Hedda?

GEORGE. Not a thing, Bertha, thank you. We'll let her sleep a little longer. You can do something for me, though: put this *(Case.)* in the attic, would you?

BERTHA. Certainly, "doctor."

GEORGE. "Doctor"! Is Miss Bertha being saucy with me?

BERTHA. *(Coyly, as she exits.)* And maybe a vet soon!

GEORGE. *(Puzzled.)* Vet?

JULIANA. We are all so very proud of you, Georgie.

GEORGE. And isn't it a shocking thing to admit — no, not shocking, embarrassing, no, not embarrassing, pathetic, really pathetic — I'm very proud of myself! You saw that case? Packed with the material for my new book. You wouldn't believe what I unearthed all over Europe — in archives, museums, private libraries — stuff people had completely forgotten was there. Absolutely incredible material!

JULIANA.   So your honeymoon wasn't all gadding about and pleasure then?

GEORGE.   Certainly not! And I want another hug! *(He hugs her.)* Sit down beside me before Hedda appears and tell me all the gossip I've missed in the past six months. Here, take your hat off. No, that was always my job, wasn't it? *(He slowly removes her hat.)*

JULIANA.   It's just as if you were still home with us.

GEORGE.   It's new, isn't it?

JULIANA.   A week old. Got it in a charity sale.

GEORGE.   Well, if Miss Juliana Tesman isn't the most elegant lady in town.

JULIANA.   I got it for Hedda — so that she won't be ashamed of me if we were to go for a walk together. *(He hugs her again quickly.)*

GEORGE.   You are a very special — a most special aunt.

JULIANA.   I think your honeymoon was the longest six months of my life. There were times when I wondered would I ever see you again!

GEORGE.   Here I am!

JULIANA.   And a married man! I have to keep telling myself: our Georgie is married to Hedda Gabler that half the men in town were mad about.

GEORGE.   I know. Lucky, lucky George Tesman.

JULIANA.   Indeed.

GEORGE.   More than lucky. Blessed. I'm blessed — amn't I?

JULIANA.   You deserve to be. But my secret hope is that you have great good news for me. Well?

GEORGE.   I gave you all my news in my letters.

JULIANA.   *Really* good news.

GEORGE.   Getting the doctorate? But I told you all that —

JULIANA.   No, no, no, no — *great* good news — you know, you and Hedda — special news, Georgie.

GEORGE.   The professorship?

JULIANA.   That's not quite what —

GEORGE.   As good as mine, Auntie Juju, if you believe the rumours.

JULIANA.   Ah.

GEORGE.   The appointment will be announced very soon. Professor George Tesman — hasn't it a ring to it?

JULIANA.   Yes.

GEORGE.   So I'll be doubly blessed, won't I?

JULIANA.   I hope so. That long honeymoon must have cost you a fortune, George?

GEORGE. Several fortunes.

JULIANA. *(Anxiously.)* It didn't, did it?

GEORGE. Joking — joking. Yes, it was expensive: my wife isn't exactly a frugal woman. But the grant covered most of — well, some of it. Don't worry. Everything is in hand.

JULIANA. Have you had a chance to look over the house yet?

GEORGE. I was up at daybreak.

JULIANA. Well?

GEORGE. The house is wonderful. The house is magnificent.

JULIANA. It's a beautiful home.

GEORGE. But what are we to do with the two extra rooms between the back door and Hedda's bedroom?

JULIANA. *(Coyly.)* Oh, you'll find a use for them — in time, George.

GEORGE. For my library! The very thing!

JULIANA. Yes, for your library.

GEORGE. Good idea, Auntie Juju. Yes, we were so lucky to get it. The only house in town Hedda always said she'd ever live in and it comes on the market as we're setting off on our honeymoon. And what do the cautious Tesmans do? Promptly buy it!

JULIANA. But a very dear house.

GEORGE. These things are all relative, aren't they? Anyhow Judge Brack got us very favourable terms. He wrote to Hedda and explained it all.

JULIANA. And I've gone security for the rugs and these bits and pieces.

GEORGE. You?

JULIANA. Why the surprise?

GEORGE. Darling Auntie Juju, you have no money.

JULIANA. Darling nephew Georgie, I have my annuity, haven't I?

GEORGE. But your annuity is the only —

JULIANA. So I raised a modest mortgage on Aunt Rena's and my trust fund.

GEORGE. But that's the only money you've got in the whole world!

JULIANA. No risk involved. A mere formality, Judge Brack assures me. And to be able to help you in any small way I can — don't you know how much pleasure that gives *me?* No father, no mother, just two ancient aunts to give you a little assistance. And look at how wonderfully you've turned out! You're a very successful young man, Dr. Tesman.

GEORGE. Am I?

JULIANA. "Am I?" A magnificent home.

GEORGE. An adorable aunt.

JULIANA. A beautiful wife.

GEORGE. Two adorable aunts.

JULIANA. A well-deserved doctorate.

GEORGE. Indeed.

JULIANA. A professorship just round the corner …

GEORGE. Yes! The question is: will George Tesman ever come down to earth again?

JULIANA. Don't be in a hurry. And where are all those rivals of yours now? All those mean-spirited contemporaries who tried to thwart every move you made? Washed up! And that most unfortunate wretch of them all, that awful libertine who seemed to overshadow everything you ever accomplished, where is *he* now?

GEORGE. *(Laughs.)* "Libertine"! The lady can't be talking about my very old friend, Eilert Loevborg, can she?

JULIANA. Friend!

GEORGE. The hugely talented Eilert Loevborg?

JULIANA. Debauchee!

GEORGE. She may be, I suspect.

JULIANA. Lying in some squalid bed of his own making — I hope.

GEORGE. *(Pretended shock.)* Auntie Juju!

JULIANA. God forgive me.

GEORGE. Yes, indeed. Have you heard anything about Loevborg in the past six months?

JULIANA. Just that he has brought out a new book.

GEORGE. *(Very shocked.)* He has not!

JULIANA. For what it's worth.

GEORGE. Eilert Loevborg — well, isn't he astonishing! A new book!

JULIANA. If anybody's interested.

GEORGE. Oh, people are very interested, Auntie Juju.

JULIANA. Now when your book comes out, then they'll sit up. *(Bertha returns.)* What's it about, George?

BERTHA. You shouldn't leave Miss Rena alone for too long.

JULIANA. Going in a moment.

GEORGE. Domestic craft and husbandry as practised in Holland and parts of Belgium in the tenth century.

JULIANA. Fascinating.

GEORGE. You're very sweet. It won't appear for a very long time. There are months of research and cataloging to be done.

JULIANA. And you're good at that. But when it does appear!

BERTHA. Miss Juliana …

JULIANA. I know — I know — I'm going, Bertha.

GEORGE. Can't wait to get at it. And in my own home.

JULIANA. And with the woman of your dreams.

GEORGE. That's the most wonderful thing ever happened to me, Juju.

JULIANA. I know.

GEORGE. Can't get over Loevborg having a new book out. Ah, Hedda! *(Hedda enters the back room. Good height, striking appearance, aristocratic face, cold, grey eyes. Dressed in an elegant dressing gown.)*

JULIANA. Good morning, dear Hedda; a very good morning.

HEDDA. Good morning to you, Miss Tesman. *(To Bertha.)* Don't you know where the kitchen is? *(To Juliana.)* An early visit, isn't it?

GEORGE. *(To Bertha as she exits.)* Thank you.

BERTHA. What's that?

GEORGE. For leaving up my case.

JULIANA. I know; far too early. I've already apologised to George. And did you sleep well in your new home?

HEDDA. Off and on.

GEORGE. "Off and — "! You were out cold when I got up.

HEDDA. New surroundings take a little getting used to, Miss Tesman.

JULIANA. Juliana — Julia — even Juju, I'm afraid.

HEDDA. So it will take some time. *(Sharply.)* Why did the maid open those windows? That sun is blinding.

JULIANA. I'll close them.

HEDDA. George, you close them. No, just pull the curtains. The atmosphere's stifling with all those flowers. *(George pulls the curtains.)*

GEORGE. There you are. Fresh air *and* shade.

HEDDA. Aren't you going to sit down, Miss Tesman?

JULIANA. I've got to get back, thank you — now that I know you're both fine. If I'm away for any length of time poor Rena gets so agitated.

GEORGE. Give her my love.

JULIANA. I will.

GEORGE. And tell her I'll be over to see her this afternoon.

JULIANA. Oh, George! I almost forgot! For you. *(From her bag she produces a package wrapped in paper.)*

GEORGE. Yes?

JULIANA. From Rena. *(Hedda busies herself taking flowers from the top of the piano and arranging them in vases on the floor.)*

GEORGE. *(Opening parcel.)* Oh, for heaven's sake, I don't believe it! Would you look at that! Look, Hedda, look! My slippers!

HEDDA. *(She does not look.)* "For heaven's sake."

GEORGE. *(To Juliana.)* She knows all about them. *(He kisses them. To Hedda.)* Aren't they magnificent?

HEDDA. From the moment he realised he'd left them behind, the honeymoon was a disaster.

GEORGE. That's unfair. But yes — yes — yes — they are very important to me. Look, Hedda — Auntie Rena's exquisite embroidery. I told you about it. Every year, as soon as my birthday came around, she would painstakingly sketch out a new wildflower and then embroider it. It might take two — three — months to finish it. There's a wake-robin. And a sea aster. And that was for my twenty-fifth — that triumphant *Cardamine pratensis* — that's a lady's smock. Look at the subtlety, the precision, of those lilac leaves. And an autumn crocus. And a shepherd's purse. All those shy greens and browns and cheeky pinks. And a white archangel. And a saucy little vetch for my eighteenth. Such skill — such artistry. Oh my goodness. This is a chronicle of my life, Hedda; a record of my deepest emotions, my most opulent memories. Look, Hedda.

HEDDA. What has it to do with me?

GEORGE. What do you — ?

HEDDA. Not my emotions, not my memories, are they?

GEORGE. No, they're not, darling. But if they're —

JULIANA. Hedda's right, George. They are very special — to you.

GEORGE. But Hedda's part of the family now and surely what is important to —

HEDDA. We've got to let that maid go, Miss Tesman.

JULIANA. Bertha?!

GEORGE. Let Bertha go?

JULIANA. Oh, Hedda ...

GEORGE. What are you saying, Hedda?

HEDDA. What sort of a sloven is she? Things lying all over the place. Flowers scattered everywhere. Look at that old hat lying here on a chair.

GEORGE. *(Gently.)* That's Auntie Juju's old hat, Hedda.

HEDDA. Ah?

JULIANA. And it's a relatively young hat.

HEDDA. *(Shrugs.)* My mistake.

JULIANA. In fact this is its first outing on *my* head.

GEORGE. And what a very, very blessed hat it is to be worn by such an elegant —

JULIANA. Don't be silly, George: hats can't be blessed — only people. *(Holds out her hand.)* My parasol if you please. Mine also, Hedda; and *brand*-new.

GEORGE. I've never seen you look more graceful, Auntie Juju. *(To Hedda.)* Isn't she graceful?

HEDDA. Lovely.

GEORGE. And you're lovely, too, Hedda. Beautiful. Beautiful without qualification. *(To Juliana.)* Isn't Hedda beautiful?

JULIANA. Hedda has always been beautiful. *(Juliana moves towards the door.)*

GEORGE. And filled out a little on our travels, hasn't she? Just a little more ample? Attractively more ample?

HEDDA. *(Sharply.)* George, please. *(Juliana stops and turns back.)*

GEORGE. She thinks that dressing gown disguises it, but I can tell you —

HEDDA. You can tell nothing at all.

GEORGE. I can, you know, I can! Of course all those enormous plates of fruit strudel we devoured in the Tyrol, they all contributed as well.

HEDDA. I'm exactly the same as I was before we went away.

GEORGE. Sorry, my darling. Just that tiny bit plumper and hugely more attractive.

HEDDA. Oh for God's sake!

GEORGE. Amn't I right, Auntie Juju? *(Juliana looks at Hedda for a few seconds.)*

JULIANA. Hedda is beautiful. Hedda is just so beautiful. *(Now she goes to Hedda, takes her head between her hands, draws it towards her, and kisses her on the forehead.)*

HEDDA. God bless you and keep you, Hedda Tesman. For George's sake. *(Hedda breaks away.)*

HEDDA. Please — please —

JULIANA. I'll come over every day to see you both.

GEORGE. Wonderful. Nobody would be more welcome. *(Juliana goes off. George goes with her. We hear him thanking her for the slippers and sending his love to Rena. Hedda paces the room in scarcely controlled fury, her arms raised above her head, her fists clenched. She flings back*

16

the curtains on the French window and stares out. George returns.)
What a sophisticated woman that is. *(He picks up the slippers.)* What
are you looking at?
HEDDA. The leaves. Yellow and withered already.
GEORGE. We *are* into September, you know.
HEDDA. I know — I know — don't I know.
GEORGE. Did you notice anything a little ... different about
Auntie Juju? A bit — I don't know — withdrawn?
HEDDA. I couldn't tell. I don't know her well enough.
GEORGE. I hope I didn't say anything wrong.
HEDDA. Maybe that episode with the hat offended her. I should
make it up with her.
GEORGE. Ah, Hedda, would you?
HEDDA. When you see them this afternoon, invite her to come
over and spend the evening with us.
GEORGE. She'd like that, I know. Thank you. And there's another
thing I know she'd really love: could you call her Auntie Juju?
HEDDA. That's a ridiculous name.
GEORGE. Is it? I'm so used to —
HEDDA. And we've discussed this before.
GEORGE. And you're one of the family now. Aunt Juliana?
HEDDA. You shouldn't ask this of me, George.
GEORGE. Just Juliana?
HEDDA. I will not be coerced.
GEORGE. For my sake, Hedda?
HEDDA. Alright — alright — alright — I'll call her Aunt. That's
as far as I'll go.
GEORGE. Very generous of you. Thank you. What's the matter?
HEDDA. My old piano. Completely out of place with these fur-
nishings.
GEORGE. As soon as my salary starts coming through we'll see
about selling it and maybe getting a new one.
HEDDA. No, no, I'm not going to part with it. I want to put it
in there *(The back room.)* and I want a new one in here.
GEORGE. I suppose we could look into it. *(She picks up a bunch
of flowers from the top of the piano.)*
HEDDA. These weren't here when we got in last night.
GEORGE. Auntie Juju probably brought them for you.
HEDDA. *(Reads card.)* "Will come back very soon. Mrs ... "
GEORGE. Who?

HEDDA. "Elvsted. Mrs. T. Elvsted."

GEORGE. Thea Elvsted! Really! Thea Rysing that used to be!

HEDDA. Thea Rysing indeed. An old flame of yours — am I right?

GEORGE. For all of a week, Hedda. Long before I knew you.

HEDDA. Haven't seen her — not since we were at school together. A "sincere" creature, I remember; and anxious, so anxious. With a mass of ridiculous golden curls that she thought were her great asset and kept flaunting them. Why is she calling on us?

GEORGE. Going off her head, I suspect, in that awful backwater she lives in — somewhere away up near Trondheim, isn't it? I remember hearing she married an elderly resident magistrate up there.

HEDDA. Didn't he move up there, too, to the Trondheim area, Eilert Loevborg?

GEORGE. D'you know, you're right! What in God's name brought him away up there?

BERTHA. She's back, madam, the lady who brought the flowers earlier.

HEDDA. Well, show her in. *(Bertha shows Thea Elvsted in and retires. Thea Elvsted is an attractive woman of slight build. A few years younger than Hedda. Her hair is abundant and golden. Her blue eyes are alert. She carries with her an air of diffidence, of vague anxiety. But behind that is a woman of resolution and determination. Hedda greets her warmly.)* Mrs. Elvsted ! Lovely to see you again.

THEA. And you, Mrs. Tesman. It has been a long time.

HEDDA. Far too long. And thank you for the flowers. They are beautiful.

THEA. You're welcome.

GEORGE. *(His hand out.)* Too long indeed, Mrs. Elvsted. Good to see you.

THEA. And very belated congratulations on your wedding. I wish you both a long and happy life together.

HEDDA. Thank you.

GEORGE. When did you get into town?

THEA. Around lunchtime yesterday. I came straight here. And when you weren't here — I can't tell you — I felt suddenly desolate, desperate almost.

HEDDA. What's the matter, Mrs. Elvsted? Here, take a seat.

THEA. It's so reassuring to be here with you both.

HEDDA. Sit down here.

THEA. I can't. I'm too —

HEDDA. *(Firmly.)* Sit here, Mrs. Elvsted. Sit. *(She draws her to the couch and sits beside her.)*

GEORGE. What is it?

HEDDA. Something's happened at home — isn't that it?

GEORGE. Maybe we can help.

HEDDA. Something to do with your husband?

THEA. No, no, not really him. Well, partly him. It's — it's — it's —

GEORGE. Take your time.

THEA. Eilert Loevborg is here.

HEDDA. *(Softly.)* Oh my God.

GEORGE. Here — in town?

THEA. For the past week.

GEORGE. D'you hear that, Hedda? Loevborg is —

HEDDA. *(Sharply.)* I heard.

THEA. Back in this treacherous environment that almost destroyed him a few years ago. And nobody to look after him. How can he survive? He can't. He'll go under again.

HEDDA. Eilert Loevborg isn't your responsibility, Mrs. Elvsted.

THEA. I know that. But he was my children's tutor, and I feel some responsibility for him. No, not my children — I don't have a family — my husband's children.

GEORGE. And was he — forgive me — I mean I wouldn't have thought Loevborg was sufficiently in control of his life to be a tutor.

THEA. He's a new man, Eilert. He has himself completely in hand now. For the past three years his behaviour has been impeccable.

GEORGE. D'you hear that, Hedda? His behaviour has been —

HEDDA. *(Sharply.)* I heard.

THEA. A complete turnaround. Eilert Loevborg is now exemplary.

HEDDA. Really?

THEA. But I'm frightened for him here, back in all the old haunts with all those sleazy hangers-on. And now with money in his pocket! He's bound to collapse again, isn't he?

GEORGE. But why didn't he stay up in Trondheim with you and your husband?

THEA. How could he? — all the excitement with the new book — strangers stopping him in the street — reporters knocking at the door — scores of letters every day. He got so excited, so agitated. How could he be held in Trondheim? He had to get to the city.

GEORGE. *(To Hedda.)* Auntie Juju mentioned something about that book.

THEA. A cultural history of Europe, no less. And an instant success when it came out a fortnight ago. It's in its fifth reprint.

GEORGE.   So this isn't a reworking of that old monograph he published seven years ago?

THEA. No, no. This is altogether new. And all done in the past eighteen months when he was living with us.

GEORGE. Well, well, well. Good for Loevborg, that's what I say. Loevborg resurrectus. Excellent news, Hedda, isn't it? *(Hedda does not respond.)*

THEA. Eilert Loevborg, the celebrated author!

HEDDA. Have you met him here in town?

THEA. I managed to find his address only this morning.

HEDDA. Why didn't your husband come down to look after him? He's your husband's friend, isn't he?

THEA. He's caught up at the assizes. Anyhow I had shopping to do.

HEDDA. *(Smiling.)* Well, of course. *(Thea rises to leave.)*

THEA. He'll certainly drop in to see you. You and he work in the same field, don't you?

GEORGE. Adjoining fields.

THEA. And he's so fond of both of you — I know that.

GEORGE. And we're really fond of Eilert. Aren't we, Hedda? *(Hedda does not respond.)*

THEA. Who can resist Eilert? My husband thinks the world of him, too. If he does drop in, you'll take care of him, won't you? Without the anchor of a home, he'll just drift.

GEORGE. Anything we can do for Eilert Loevborg — anything in the world — we'll be happy to do it.

HEDDA. Don't be stupid! Eilert Loevborg isn't going to "drop in" on us! The man's on the rampage for God's sake — triumphant, delirious with sudden success! He's being toasted by scores of old and new friends. Even as we sit here he's probably painting the town … scarlet!

THEA. You don't think that he's already — ?

HEDDA. Do you expect him to tear himself away from that wonderful delirium and "drop in" on this drab anchorage? Well, do you?

THEA. So you think he's already lost?

HEDDA. I think — if you want to save him from himself —

THEA. I must. Nobody else can. When he gets into one of those manic moods he's capable of doing himself real damage.

HEDDA. Then we must get him up here this very day. George

will write to him.

GEORGE. Good idea, Hedda.

THEA. Would you?

GEORGE. Of course — of course.

THEA. Here is his address.

HEDDA. And the quicker, the better.

GEORGE. I'll write him just now.

HEDDA. A formal invitation; but make it very warm. You *do* want him to come, George, don't you? *(George pauses briefly.)*

GEORGE. Why wouldn't I want Eilert to come? *(He goes to the door. Pauses.)* My slippers. *(He takes his slippers and exits.)*

THEA. *(Calling.)* Don't say anything about me having asked you. *(He puts his fingers to his lips and disappears.)* I pray to God he comes, Mrs. Tesman.

HEDDA. Yes, he'll come. You're too anxious; get a hold of yourself. And now we've got George out of the way we can really talk. Sit down here beside me. *(They sit together on the sofa. Hedda takes Thea's hand in hers.)*

THEA. I'll have to go very soon, Mrs. Tesman.

HEDDA. "Mrs. Tesman — Mrs. Tesman"! I'm sick of damn convention. It's Hedda — Hedda! Weren't we at school together? You knew me as Hedda and I knew you as Thea.

THEA. You were a year ahead of me.

HEDDA. Yes, about that.

THEA. I was terrified of you.

HEDDA. Thea!

THEA. When we met on the stair, you used to pull my hair.

HEDDA. Wasn't I a little brat!

THEA. And you told me once you'd like to set fire to it.

HEDDA. *(Laughs.)* I never did!

THEA. You meant it, too.

HEDDA. Oh my God, what a demon I must have been!

THEA. I really *was* terrified of you.

HEDDA. Can you ever forgive me?

THEA. And then you were the daughter of General Gabler and my father was a storeman on the docks. That was another chasm. Anyhow … a long time ago … I really must leave.

HEDDA. No, no, you can't leave now, Thea. Wait until George writes his letter. Things haven't been going so well at home, have they?

THEA. I'd rather not talk about that.

HEDDA. You haven't forgiven me. Oh, Thea. *(Kisses Thea's cheek.)* I am sorry. How can I make it up to you?

THEA. What is there to make up?

HEDDA. You're not accustomed to kindness, Thea, are you? Even at home?

THEA. I haven't got a home. I never had a home.

HEDDA. You have the Elvsted home.

THEA. Just an address.

HEDDA. You first went there as a housekeeper, didn't you?

THEA. I was employed as a governess. But his wife — his late wife — became very ill and eventually was invalided and I had to look after all the household affairs as well.

HEDDA. And you ended up mistress of the house?

THEA. Yes.

HEDDA. And then you and Mr. Elvsted got married?

THEA. Five years ago.

HEDDA. And wasn't Eilert Loevborg up there the last three years?

THEA. Yes.

HEDDA. Had you known him before that?

THEA. Not really. I knew *of* him of course.

HEDDA. So he stayed in the Elvsted house?

THEA. I couldn't do the teaching and manage the household.

HEDDA. So he took on the tutoring job?

THEA. Yes.

HEDDA. And I suppose your husband has to be away a lot?

THEA. He has a huge area to cover; a great deal of travelling.

HEDDA. So much was left to you then: the usual anxieties of the bourgeoisie — the children's studies — and their grinds — and the household routine — and the difficulty of getting staff. And your husband — is he a considerate man? Is he a good provider? Is he faithful?

THEA. Oh yes, yes.

HEDDA. Is he kind to you?

THEA. He probably thinks he is.

HEDDA. He's a lot older than you, isn't he?

THEA. More than twenty years. We have nothing at all in common.

HEDDA. Does he love you?

THEA. Does he? Maybe. In his own way. I'm useful. I'm cheap. I don't know if he cares about anybody. His children, perhaps.

HEDDA. He cares about Eilert Loevborg, Thea.

THEA. What do you mean?

HEDDA. As you say, "Who can resist Eilert?" And he did send you down to look after him.

THEA. Not at all. He was away at assizes somewhere. He doesn't even know I'm here. I just couldn't stay up there alone, Hedda. So I threw some things in a bag and walked out. I think I was hysterical.

HEDDA. Not a word to anyone?

THEA. I ran all the way to the station. I think I was demented.

HEDDA. That was a very courageous thing to do, Thea.

THEA. I don't think I had a choice.

HEDDA. But what will your husband say when you go back?

THEA. I'm never going back there again.

HEDDA. You've left your husband, your home — your anchor — for good? And in broad daylight?

THEA. Yes.

HEDDA. So *you're* drifting now, Thea?

THEA. Yes.

HEDDA. And you don't care about a scandal, what people will say about you?

THEA. Not really. Not at all, I think.

HEDDA. How I envy you that courage. I wish to God I could summon that daring.

THEA. Not courage, is it? I don't think I had a choice.

HEDDA. Oh yes, I envy you, Thea Elvsted. *(She kisses Thea again on the cheek. Pause. Very brisk:)* And now I want to know all about you and Eilert Loevborg — step by step — Thea and Eilert — every detail.

THEA. Thea and Eilert ... I tell myself it has a special euphony.

HEDDA. And it has. Now. Step by step.

THEA. Thea and Eilert ... yes ... I used to watch him through a crack in the parlour door; teaching the children at the big, mahogany table. The stooped shoulders. The patient hands. The lank hair. But especially the face; and the cornflower blue eyes, those hesitant, irresolute eyes that hinted at weakness. And always, always that wan, apologetic smile that confirmed that weakness. Flinching before the sly bullying of the children and my husband's crude discourtesies. I could see how damaged he was and how incapable of protecting himself: that every lesson with the children and every encounter with my husband was an occasion for humiliation. And watching him through a crack in the parlour door I suddenly

knew that I loved that weak, talented, damaged Eilert Loevborg ...
yes. Loved him suddenly and fiercely and altogether without caution. A love so fierce and so palpable that I knew it could shelter him
from some of those humiliations and retrieve that loss of confidence
and indeed fortify him against the pull of those old excesses, just
because it was so fierce a love, because it was so palpable. And that's
what I did. I loved him away from his dissipations. I loved him into
an accord with himself again. I even loved him into reciprocating
my love for him. And so step by step he became more resolute. And
step by step the apologetic smile disappeared and he began to laugh
again. And with his new self-belief he began to educate me; opened
me up just by talking to me and encouraging me to respond to
him; taught me to look for different choices and fresh possibilities.
And so we rescued one another. I really believed that. I know I felt
I had been delivered. I think he felt redeemed too. Eilert Loevborg
... yes ... And then one day he asked me — out of the blue — he
asked me would I help him with the new book he was planning to
write, to write it *with* him. And I shocked myself — "Of course I
will," I said. Me! The housekeeper, the daughter of the storeman
on the docks! And that's what we did, Hedda: we wrote that book
together; six hours a day for eighteen months. "Collaborators" —
that was his name for us. And during that eighteen months I dis-
covered that our deliverance was more than just a liberation. It had
within it an approval, maybe even a benediction on what we were
doing together: Thea and Eilert, collaborators ... And that's it,
Hedda: step by step. No, I have left out a step. There is a dancer-
singer-performer back in town. A creature with blazing red hair. A
hussy. Eilert and she were friends once — well, acquaintances. He
hasn't seen her in years. She wrote to him last week. The letter, I
know, upset him. Apparently she carries a pistol in her handbag.
And when they parted years ago, she threatened to shoot him.

HEDDA. People don't do that sort of thing. *(George approaches.
She whispers:)* Strictly between you and me.

THEA. Oh yes, Hedda, please, please.

HEDDA. Not a word.

GEORGE. Here we are. Formal but *very* warm.

HEDDA. Mrs. Elvsted is about to leave, George. I'll walk her to
the garden gate.

GEORGE. Would you ask Bertha to see to this? *(Letter.)*

HEDDA. *(Takes envelope.)* I'll tell her. *(Bertha enters.)* Drop this in the post, Berna.

BERTHA. Judge Brack is here to see you both.

HEDDA. Show him in. And post that letter immediately.

BERTHA. Yes, madam. *(Bertha shows Brack in and then exits. Brack is in his mid-forties. Elegantly dressed; a little vain; a little pompous. He is fastidious — almost precious — in his manner and speech. He is very aware that he presents this image of himself and there is a salutary undertone of self-mockery in the presentation. He prides himself in his knowledge of this new slang and these American neologisms. At the same time he uses this vocabulary with a hint of derision. He appears to be very relaxed but the mind is razor-sharp and the alert eyes miss nothing.)*

BRACK. I know — I know — an unconscionable hour to call on people of feeling. Assure me I *am* welcome.

HEDDA. Always, Judge Brack. *(He kisses her hand with — almost — mock formality.)*

BRACK. The most elegant Mrs. Tesman.

HEDDA. And this is Mrs. Elvsted. Judge Brack.

BRACK. *(Bows.)* Enchanté.

THEA. *(Ill at ease.)* If you'll excuse me, Hedda —

HEDDA. You look different by daylight, Your Honour.

BRACK. Really? Should that disquiet me?

HEDDA. You look even younger.

BRACK. Mrs. Tesman is elegant *and* artful.

GEORGE. And how do you think she *(Hedda.)* looks, Judge? Did you notice she has put on a little —

BRACK. Much too early in the day to take cognisance of mere appearances.

HEDDA. Have you thanked the judge for all the trouble he went to for us?

GEORGE. I was about to.

BRACK. Nothing — nothing. My pleasure.

HEDDA. What we would have done without you, I just don't know.

THEA. Sorry for fussing, but I'm afraid I have to go.

BRACK. I'm interrupting something, am I?

THEA. No, no, don't think that — nothing at all — please don't think that. Hedda will tell you I was about to —

HEDDA. Yes, she's anxious to get away.

THEA. *(To Brack.)* Very pleased to meet you. I hope we meet again very … soon.

BRACK. As do I.

THEA. Goodbye, George.

GEORGE. The flowers are lovely.

THEA. Congratulations again. *(Thea and Hedda exit.)*

BRACK. You've had a look around. Is your lady wife happy with it all?

GEORGE. Thank you *so* much. Everything's just perfect.

BRACK. Splendid.

GEORGE. We'll probably move things round a bit.

BRACK. Of course.

GEORGE. And she tells me she still has a few more items she has to buy.

BRACK. *(Concerned.)* Items?

GEORGE. God knows what. Nothing for you to be concerned about. Have a seat.

BRACK. There is something I think we should talk about, George.

GEORGE. Money.

BRACK. Good Lord no! We can anguish over that later. Though I do wish the furnishings were a little more … demure.

GEORGE. Impossible, Judge. You know Hedda — anything more modest and she would just wilt.

BRACK. *(Wryly.)* Really?

GEORGE. And when the professorship comes through we'll be comfortably on top of our finances again.

BRACK. These matters take time, Tesman.

GEORGE. Have you heard something?

BRACK. Nothing reliable … rumours … gossip. Yes, I did hear one bit of interesting tattle: your old friend, Eilert Loevborg, is back in town.

GEORGE. So Mrs. Elvsted told me.

BRACK. Mrs.…?

GEORGE. Elvsted. The magistrate's wife. You've just met her.

BRACK. Of course. A lady addicted to her anxieties, I suspect.

GEORGE. *(Laughs.)* Is she? Anyhow Loevborg has been living with the Elvsteds in the outskirts of Trondheim.

BRACK. And turned over a new leaf, would you believe.

GEORGE. He has!

BRACK. A completely reformed character, they say.

GEORGE. Yes!

BRACK. Like our friend, Saint Paul. But I'm afraid my dubious trade has taught me to be wary of sudden conversions.

GEORGE. And he has a new book out. Everybody's talking about it.

BRACK. So I hear.

GEORGE. A huge popular success, apparently.

BRACK. I'll be candid with you, George: I never did believe in Paul's conversion. I mean, tumbling off a horse and all that circus stuff ... Quite improbable.

GEORGE. *(Laughs.)* Judge!

BRACK. Loevborg's new book? Oh yes, an enormous success. "Jumbo," as I'm told the Americans have it. Jumbo — rather sweet, isn't it?

GEORGE. He's such a gifted man. And only a few years ago everyone had written him off. He should make some money on this. But the question is: when this fuss dies down, what will he live on? *(Hedda enters.)*

HEDDA. George's persistent worry about everybody: "What will he live on?" What will who live on?

GEORGE. Poor old Loevborg. The money his uncle left him a few years ago, that must be long gone. And he can't produce a new book every year. So what will become of him?

HEDDA. Or any of us.

GEORGE. Sorry?

BRACK. He has relatives in the town who still have a lot of clout. *(To himself.)* "Clout" — sounds like an Americanism, too, doesn't it?

GEORGE. They've washed their hands of him.

BRACK. Their golden boy?

GEORGE. Haven't spoken to him in years.

BRACK. Say what you like, he *has* produced a successful book.

HEDDA. So then Elvsted was right: she *has* delivered him. *(Pause.)*

BRACK. *(Pretended confusion.)* Where to?

HEDDA. *(Laughs.)* Rescued him, Judge! redeemed him! Loevborg is *saved. (Brack crosses his arms before his face to ward off evil.)*

BRACK. Saved?! Oh good God! That word terrifies me! I will not have it!

HEDDA. You shouldn't worry. It's not something you're likely to experience.

GEORGE. Well, maybe they'll find something for him. He is such a brilliant man. By the way, Hedda, I've asked him over to dinner this evening.

BRACK. But you're coming to my bachelor party this evening. I

27

invited you down at the quay last night.

HEDDA. Had you forgotten, George?

GEORGE. Sorry — I'm afraid I did — my apologies — I really am sorry, Judge.

BRACK. Don't worry. Loevborg won't turn up here.

HEDDA. Why won't he? *(Brack gets to his feet.)*

BRACK. There's something both of you ought to know.

GEORGE. About Eilert?

BRACK. About Eilert. About you, too. The professorship — the actual appointment — may not come through as easily or as quickly as we hoped. In fact I'm told they've decided to advertise the post again. So the job may well attract many new applicants.

HEDDA. Like Loevborg?

BRACK. Indeed.

GEORGE. Oh my goodness, do you hear that, Hedda?

HEDDA. *(Softly. Immobile.)* Interesting.

GEORGE. But this is outrageous! For God's sake, I was practically promised that job! I've just got married! I got married on the strength of that job! We've got huge debts! And we've borrowed money from Auntie Juju!

BRACK. And I expect you'll get it. You'll just have to take part in a competition.

HEDDA. *(Softly. Immobile.)* It will be a kind of duel, won't it?

GEORGE. How can you be so damned calm, Hedda?

HEDDA. I can hardly wait for the outcome.

BRACK. Anyhow it's just as well you know how things stand, Mrs. Tesman — before you decide on buying any extra items.

HEDDA. My plans won't change, Judge.

BRACK. Probably not. Knowing you. And now I must leave you. *(To George.)* I'll pick you up this evening on my way home from my walk.

GEORGE. *(Confused.)* Yes — please — yes — do that if you would — forgive me, I'm a little …

HEDDA. Goodbye, Judge. I'll see you later.

BRACK. Au revoir. I'm wrong — it's not an Americanism, "clout." An archery term — the mark shot at — a fair clout. Glad I got that. Until this evening. *(He exits.)*

GEORGE. He's making all that up, isn't he? — about a competition. Just to keep me on my toes, isn't it? Dear God, I'm shattered, Hedda. Look — I'm shaking. He's right: the job's gone, isn't it? It is, isn't it? Yes, it's gone. Was it all a fantasy? It just shows, you can't live out your daydreams, doesn't it?

HEDDA. Is that what you're doing?

GEORGE. I don't know. Is it? Got married; bought our dream house; furnished it stylishly — all on an expectation. It wasn't all a daydream, Hedda, was it?

HEDDA. We agreed to live in a certain style.

GEORGE. We did, didn't we? And I wanted all that so much, really for you, only for you: a splendid house, a circle of close friends, and at the heart of it all, my Hedda, my beautiful, translucent Hedda. I'm sorry, my love. This isn't what you deserve.

HEDDA. So no butler?

GEORGE. *(Bleak laugh.)* No butler.

HEDDA. And the bay mare you promised me?

GEORGE. Oh God no, Hedda. Sorry. The cost and upkeep —

HEDDA. Well, I have at least one thing to amuse me.

GEORGE. What's that?

HEDDA. My father's pistols.

GEORGE. *(Alarmed.)* Pistols?

HEDDA. The pistols General Gabler left me. *(As she exits:)*

GEORGE. *(Calling.)* For heaven's sake, Hedda, don't even touch those awful things. Please, love. For my sake, darling … Oh my goodness …

End of Act One

ACT TWO

Tesman's drawing room, early afternoon of the same day. The piano is gone and in its place an elegant writing table and a bookcase. Most of the flowers have been removed.

Mrs. Elvsted's bouquet now sits in the centre of the table. Hedda is alone onstage, standing beside the open French windows. She is loading a pistol. There is an identical pistol in the open pistol case on the table. Hedda is wearing a beautiful dress.

HEDDA. *(Looking out.)* Judge Brack, if you don't mind!

BRACK. *(Offstage.)* It is indeed, Mrs. Tesman.

HEDDA. Back again, Your Honour.

BRACK. *(Offstage.)* A man of my word. *(She raises the pistol and takes aim.)*

HEDDA. You're right in my sights, Judge Brack.

BRACK. *(Offstage.)* Sorry?

HEDDA. I'm about to take a shot at you.

BRACK. *(Offstage.)* Don't point that thing at me!

HEDDA. This will teach you not to slip in the back way. *(She fires.)*

BRACK. Jesus Christ, woman! Are you out of your mind?

HEDDA. I think I missed.

BRACK. *(Offstage.)* Stop that at once, Hedda! D'you hear me? At once!

HEDDA. Aren't you coming in? *(He enters through the French windows. He is very angry. He is wearing a dress suit for his bachelor party. Hat. Coat. Gloves.)* Your Honour's looking very dashing this evening.

BRACK. What do you think you're doing, woman? What in God's name are you shooting at?

HEDDA. You. The great blue sky. Whatever. It's only a game, Judge. *(He takes the gun from her hand.)*

BRACK. If you don't mind, Mrs. Tesman. That's criminal behaviour. Where's the case? *(He puts the gun away.)*

HEDDA. Just passing the time. You can be such a churl.

BRACK. Enough of that little game for today. Where's George?

HEDDA. The moment he finished lunch off he scampered to the aunties'. You're early, aren't you?

BRACK. Had I known he wasn't here I would have come even earlier.

HEDDA. And there would have been no one to receive you.

BRACK. Just you alone.

HEDDA. I have been up in my bedroom all afternoon, dressing.

BRACK. Couldn't I at least have … considered you through a crack in your bedroom door?

HEDDA. There is no crack in the bedroom door, Judge.

BRACK. You'll have to rectify that, won't you?

HEDDA. George won't be home for some time. You'll have to be patient.

BRACK. I'm a man of almost saintly patience. Let's have a talk, you and I.

HEDDA. We haven't had a real talk for ages.

BRACK. You mean *à deux?*

HEDDA. I believe I do.

BRACK. You were away so long, Hedda, I was beginning to despair of ever seeing you again.

HEDDA. I thought myself I'd never get back.

BRACK. From your exciting honeymoon?

HEDDA. *(Ironically.)* Thrilling.

BRACK. George found it exciting — according to his letters.

HEDDA. Burrowing into archives, grubbling around old libraries, copying out old documents faithfully, faithfully — that's the only thing that excites George.

BRACK. That *is* his profession.

HEDDA. I can't tell you how bored I was.

BRACK. Come on!

HEDDA. I know it sounds abnormal, but my honeymoon bored me. Am I unnatural?

BRACK. *(Laughs.)* You?!

HEDDA. Bored — bored — bored.

BRACK. I'm secretly delighted of course. But you just can't have been bored for the entire six months?

HEDDA. Have you any idea what it's like not to meet even one other person you could have a conversation with during that entire time?

BRACK. None.

HEDDA. Or the purgatory of spending the twenty-four hours of every single day with the same person?

BRACK. Hell. *(Quickly.)* Forgive me — forgive me. George Tesman is an upright and thoroughly decent man — and a worthy academic, I'm sure. I have considerable respect for George Tesman.

HEDDA. "Considerable — " You know, you practice your little cruelties very skillfully.

BRACK. Goes with the job. But, Hedda, you married the man, so you must have loved him.

HEDDA. That's sentimental.

BRACK. You *did* marry him.

HEDDA. Who could resist domestic crafts in tenth-century Holland and cottage industries in east Belgium? For God's sake, man! Yes, I did marry him — is that altogether bizarre?

BRACK. Yes, there was a time when it did look as if George was going to be a great academic star. We all believed that.

HEDDA. That's not why I married him. That didn't interest me. I married him because I had danced myself to a standstill. Because — may I be melodramatic, Judge? — because I had an instinct things had come to an end for me, that it was all played out. So in panic, despair maybe, I latched on to what was stable and dependable.

BRACK. Stable and dependable George Tesman.

HEDDA. By God he is.

BRACK. And quite a decent scholar, I'm assured. Don't overlook that.

HEDDA. And not at all ridiculous?

BRACK. What a strange word to use, Hedda. No, no, wouldn't say ridiculous.

HEDDA. An anchor then?

BRACK. Oh yes, an anchor.

HEDDA. And since he genuinely wanted to take care of me, why wouldn't I allow him? That's not what my other men friends had in mind.

BRACK. I'm sure we all cared deeply for you, Hedda.

HEDDA. Caring for me was never uppermost in your mind, Judge.

BRACK. Constantly. And I ask nothing more from life than a small group of people I can trust and hold dear and can help when help is needed and into whose houses I can come and go as freely as I wish — as a friend.

HEDDA. Of the husband?

BRACK. The wife preferably. But don't misunderstand me: my respect for the institution of marriage borders on the sacred.

HEDDA. Judge!

BRACK. In theory.

HEDDA. You're a scamp, Judge Brack.

BRACK. Me?

HEDDA. A rogue.

BRACK. Am I?

HEDDA. A smooth scoundrel.

BRACK. Never.

HEDDA. And maybe even malevolent at heart.

BRACK. Humiliate me. Enjoy your little jape. Alright, I will confess to one small vice — no, no, vice is a judgmental word; a little weakness, a minor delinquency; indeed some people find it a fetching weakness.

HEDDA. Confess.

BRACK. I must have the companionship and the consolations of women very regularly. It's a most pressing exigency. It's the only passion of my youth that has stayed faithful to me, thank heaven. Yes, I do believe that this domestic triangle arrangement can be enriching for everybody. Answer me truthfully: when you were on those interminable train journeys in Austria — those dreary forests, that dreary food, those dreary people, those execrable peasant costumes they *will* exhibit themselves in — wouldn't you have bartered something you really cherished for a little naughty prattle — *soupçon* of salacious gossip?

HEDDA. I would have bartered everything.

BRACK. Well, dear Mrs. Tesman, the honeymoon's over.

HEDDA. It's not, you know. The train has only stopped at a station.

BRACK. So jump off and stretch your legs.

HEDDA. I'm not the jumping sort.

BRACK. In the dark vault of their hearts all women are jumpers.

HEDDA. Far too cautious to jump. There's always somebody spying on you, carrying stories back. So I'll stay in the compartment — just chatting — *à deux*.

BRACK. Not at all safe and altogether miserable.

HEDDA. Too frightened to jump; terrified of scandal.

BRACK. And suppose a friend were to join you in the compartment?

A trusted friend, one of a small group?

HEDDA. That's very different.

BRACK. A desperately weak man?

HEDDA. But a fetching weakness.

BRACK. Totally unsafe and exceedingly naughty?

HEDDA. Yes, that would be different.

BRACK. That would interest you?

HEDDA. No jumping expected?

BRACK. No jumping, no melodrama, and certainly no pistols.

HEDDA. That could well be attractive, Judge Brack. *(The sound of the door opening.)*

BRACK. *(Softly.)* I do believe the triangle is complete, Miss Hedda. And completion is a satisfaction in itself, isn't it?

HEDDA. *(Softly.)* And the train moves on. *(George enters, perspiring, laden with books and academic journals.)*

GEORGE. It's very hot out there, Hedda. And these things weigh a ton. *(Sees Brack.)* Judge, you're here! Why didn't Bertha tell me?

BRACK. Came in the back way.

GEORGE. I'm not late, am I?

BRACK. I'm early.

GEORGE. I have time for a wash then. I'm sweating, lugging these all over town.

HEDDA. What have you got?

GEORGE. New publications that appeared while our backs were turned. Sneaked out, you could say. And a heap of academic journals and monographs and lectures and essays.

BRACK. All to do with your special subject?

GEORGE. Be away for even a short time and they seem to plot behind your back.

HEDDA. You must have a surfeit of that stuff.

GEORGE. All vital if you want to stay on top. And look, Hedda, Loevborg's new book. Dipped into it in the bookshop. Would you like to look at it?

HEDDA. Not now. Later. Maybe.

BRACK. And what's your verdict, Tesman, as an expert yourself?

GEORGE. A remarkable accomplishment, balanced, well organised, persuasively argued. But what's really interesting is that it's written in a light and clean style that's altogether new for Loevborg.

BRACK. Gee whiz — as the Americans have it.

GEORGE. Full of surprises is our Eilert, isn't he?

BRACK. *(To Hedda.)* Light and clean — part of his deliverance, perhaps?

GEORGE. He is an astonishing creature. I'll go and freshen up. *(To Brack.)* We don't have to dash off just now?

BRACK. No hurry.

GEORGE. *(To Hedda.)* By the way Auntie Juju won't be coming over this evening.

HEDDA. Still sulking about that hat business?

GEORGE. Oh no. How could you think that of her, Hedda? No, it's Auntie Rena. She's still very ill.

HEDDA. She usually is.

GEORGE. Yes, but this looks like a serious turn.

HEDDA. Then of course the other one must stay with her. I'll just have to make do without her, won't I?

GEORGE. She sends you her love. And she was so pleased to see how nicely you've filled out.

HEDDA. *(Icily.)* Was she?

GEORGE. *(Coyly, to Brack.)* She keeps studying Hedda for — you know — telltale symptoms. All very innocent and that little bit daring.

HEDDA. *(Softly.)* Interfering bitch. *(George exits.)*

BRACK. Temper, Miss Hedda. What's this hat business?

HEDDA. "Auntie Juju" left her hat on the chair this morning. *(Smiling.)* I pretended I thought it was the maid's.

BRACK. So you practise your own little cruelties?

HEDDA. Yes. And more frequently. And with more relish. Should that worry me, Judge?

BRACK. A pinch of malevolence gives life an interesting tang.

HEDDA. Every so often a dark impulse takes hold of me. I feel I've actually been invaded and taken over — *(Smiles.)* It's called possession in the Bible, isn't it?

BRACK. *(Shrugs.)* Wouldn't know.

HEDDA. Sometimes it's just a capricious force — poor Auntie Juju got only a tiny scratch. But it's becoming bitter and cruel. While it possesses me, I'm not responsible for anything I say or do. A sort of joyless freedom. Afterwards of course I loathe myself. A little frightening, isn't it?

BRACK. I find most women can be a little ... capricious.

HEDDA. You're playing with me, Judge.

BRACK. Sorry.

HEDDA. When it controls me, I find I even seek out my quarry. And the most vulnerable prey and the one I'm most fearful of hurting — you probably won't believe this — I'm most fearful of damaging George.

BRACK. George, the anchor. Decent George Tesman. I wouldn't be concerned for George, Hedda. That kind of simple decency has an immunity of its own. But what can I say to you? It's probably a passing mood. Marriage can be traumatic, especially for a woman of such fiercely independent spirit. Try to focus on all the good things — all the happy things around you.

HEDDA. *(Sharply.)* What are all the good and happy things around me?

BRACK. You have a beautiful home, the house you set your heart on.

HEDDA. That damned fiction has hardened into fact.

BRACK. You didn't want this house?

HEDDA. What happened was this. All last summer George used to walk me home from dances and —

BRACK. My house lay in the opposite direction; pity.

HEDDA. Your interests lay in another direction, too, Judge.

BRACK. Saucy. Anyhow — ?

HEDDA. Anyhow we were passing this house one night and George had run out of something to talk about — literally he had nothing more to say — he couldn't speak. So to help him out of his misery I pointed up to this place and off the top of my head I said there was nowhere else in the whole world I'd rather live than here. One of those capricious impulses.

BRACK. And that was it?

HEDDA. The fantasy was born.

BRACK. So you don't give a curse about this place?

HEDDA. Not a single curse. It reeks of lavender and dried flowers — like a funeral parlour.

BRACK. And after all the work we did to bedizen it for you. Part of your trouble, young lady, is that you have nothing to think about except yourself. What you must do is take up something that would engage you fully. Have you any interest in painting?

HEDDA. *(Savagely.)* The judge means a hobby! Oh, clever Judge Brack! No, painting doesn't interest me. But what about that old Turkish craft of macramé? Or beekeeping perhaps? Or collecting miniature lead soldiers? Surely that would have a special interest for a general's daughter?

BRACK. Of course we're going to be bored if we keep brooding on our little restricted lives. Look outside yourself and beyond these confines and —

HEDDA. He's so wise. We're liable to implode just because we don't see that perfect little petunia out there, or the chaste moon peeping out from behind that cloud, or the smile on baby's face when it hears its darling mummy.

BRACK. Isn't it possible — indeed very probable — that a certain happy event will alter the whole tenor of your life here?

HEDDA. That silly stuff about the professorship? Doesn't interest me in the —

BRACK. I mean you may suddenly find yourself — as most young brides do — being handed the wonderful and exciting responsibility —

HEDDA. Judge Brack has joined the coy brigade! "Isn't she filling out interestingly?" Good God, the man's actually smirking!

BRACK. But it *is* more than likely.

HEDDA. Never! D'you hear me? Never! Give me miniature soldiers any day — leaden soldiers! Ah, the professor. *(George enters. He is dressed formally for Brack's party.)*

GEORGE. No sign of Loevborg yet?

HEDDA. No.

GEORGE. He should be here soon.

BRACK. If he's coming.

GEORGE. Oh yes, he'll come. *(To Brack.)* And what you said about him this morning is just gossip. Auntie Juju says he wouldn't dare block my promotion again.

BRACK. Then everything is … hunky-dory.

GEORGE. When does your party begin, Judge?

BRACK. Nobody will turn up until seven — seven-thirty. We're in no hurry.

HEDDA. You don't have to wait around here on my account. I'll have Loevborg and Mrs. Elvsted.

BRACK. *(To George. Softly.)* Mrs. — ?

GEORGE. *(Softly back.)* Addicted-to-her-anxieties Thea.

BRACK. Ah.

HEDDA. We'll chatter and laugh and drink strong Darjeeling tea.

BRACK. Tea is sensible. Mr. Loevborg might be advised to avoid my domicile.

HEDDA. Why?

BRACK. Haven't you always averred that only men of iron discipline and heroic virtue should be allowed into my parties?

HEDDA. Then Eilert Loevborg qualifies on both counts.

BRACK. Has he — ?

HEDDA. I told you, Judge — *saved. (Brack crosses his arms before his face — to ward off evil.)*

BRACK. *(Pretended terror.)* Good God yes, you did! *(Bertha enters.)*

BERTHA. There's a gentleman here to see you, Mrs. Tesman.

GEORGE. Loevborg! You see!

HEDDA. *(To Bertha.)* Show him in.

BRACK. Does he have a halo?

HEDDA. Careful.

BRACK. Haloes make me queasy.

HEDDA. Careful.

GEORGE. I knew he'd come. All gossip, Judge. *(Eilert Loevborg enters. He is about the same age as Tesman but looks older and is slightly haggard. He speaks softly. He seems ill at ease.)* Eilert! After all these years! Welcome!

LOEVBORG. Thank you for your warm letter. *(Hand out.)* Mrs. Tesman.

HEDDA. Yes, you're most welcome.

LOEVBORG. I haven't seen you since your big day. Congratulations to you both.

HEDDA. Thank you. You know Judge Brack?

LOEVBORG. We've met.

BRACK. It has been some time.

GEORGE. And you're moving back into town again? Excellent! You must come and go in this house as freely as you wish. Mustn't he, Hedda?

HEDDA. He'll have his own place.

GEORGE. And I got your new book this afternoon. Well done! Can't wait to get stuck into it.

LOEVBORG. Don't bother. It's not serious.

GEORGE. Come on, Eilert!

LOEVBORG. I mean that. Potboiler stuff.

BRACK. It's a big success, as you know.

LOEVBORG. That's what I set out to write: a welcoming book, no demands whatever.

BRACK. You certainly succeeded, a huge success. I'm all for … jumbo.

LOEVBORG. I wanted to get my name back up there again.

BRACK. Don't we all want to be embraced? *(To Hedda.)* And nobody more than lonely judges.

GEORGE. Don't listen to that. I've dipped into it and I got a whiff of something very engaging.

LOEVBORG. Bogus all the same.

HEDDA. Don't be so stern with yourself. The public isn't nearly as austere as you.

LOEVBORG. But I *do* know, Mrs. Tesman. *(He produces a large envelope.)* Now this is the real thing.

GEORGE. *(Shocked.)* Not another new book?

LOEVBORG. Yes. The authentic thing. The genuine article. This is my important book. *(Suddenly embarrassed.)* At least it's not as easy to see through this one.

BRACK. Congratulations, sir.

GEORGE. Congratulations indeed, Eilert.

BRACK. What a fecund young man! Two books back-to-back! As we say, jeepers creepers!

GEORGE. What is this one about?

LOEVBORG. It's a sequel.

GEORGE. To what?

LOEVBORG. The last one — the one that's just out.

GEORGE. But the one that's just out — doesn't that take us right up to the present?

LOEVBORG. This one goes beyond that.

GEORGE. What do you mean, Eilert?

LOEVBORG. This one reaches into the future.

GEORGE. So it's speculative — a kind of divination?

LOEVBORG. Not really. It's made up of two parts. The first part analyses the role and the power of the arts in our society today.

GEORGE. *(Leafing through the manuscript.)* This isn't your writing, is it?

LOEVBORG. I dictated it. And the second part, the core of the book, looks at the way this society will develop under these artistic pressures.

GEORGE. *(Barely concealed dejection.)* Astonishing, Eilert! Well done. I could never tackle anything on that scale.

LOEVBORG. I thought I might read a few pages to you this evening ... just to give you a taste ... perhaps?

GEORGE. That would be great. But this evening, I'm afraid —

LOEVBORG. Of course — of course — some other time —

BRACK. We're having a small dinner party at my place this evening —

LOEVBORG. — doesn't matter —

BRACK. — to celebrate the groom's return.

LOEVBORG. Lovely.

BRACK. Would you like to join us?

LOEVBORG. *(Firmly.)* No, I can't do that. Thank you.

BRACK. Just a gathering of friends anticipating a few simple pleasures, and not, as Mrs. Tesman insists, hell-bent on debauchery.

LOEVBORG. Maybe another time.

BRACK. You could read your manuscript to Tesman at my place.

GEORGE. Good idea.

BRACK. Big house; plenty room.

GEORGE. Yes! What do you say, Eilert?

HEDDA. Mr. Loevborg doesn't want to go, George. He'll stay here and have a simple supper with me and Mrs. Elvsted. *(To Loevborg.)* Is that alright?

LOEVBORG. I'd love to. Thank you. Mrs. Elvsted is coming here? I ran into her this afternoon.

HEDDA. Yes. The three of us will have a miniature debauch here. *(Hedda rings for Bertha. When Bertha enters, Hedda whispers instructions to her. Bertha exits. Meanwhile:)*

GEORGE. And they tell me in the bookshop you're going to do a series of readings from your new book.

LOEVBORG. In the autumn. That's the plan.

GEORGE. That'll be a very successful tour.

BRACK. Excerpts from … jumbo?

GEORGE. *(Puzzled.)* Sorry?

LOEVBORG. You don't mind, do you?

GEORGE. No, no, no. Why should I mind?

LOEVBORG. I won't cut across your plans in any way?

GEORGE. I can't expect you to cancel everything just because —

LOEVBORG. If you like, I can wait until after you've been appointed professor.

GEORGE. But we're competing against one another, aren't we?

LOEVBORG. No, no, you take the professorship.

GEORGE. Me?

LOEVBORG. Why not? I've no interest in it now.

GEORGE. Eilert, you're not serious?

LOEVBORG. Very serious. I'll be happy with a *succes d'estime.*

GEORGE. You mean you're not — ?

LOEVBORG. I've withdrawn my name.

GEORGE. *(Softly.)* Gaudeamus! Auntie Juju was right, Hedda! Eilert isn't going to stand in our way!

HEDDA. *Our* way? Nothing to do with me, has it? *(Hedda goes to the back room where Bertha is putting glasses and a jug on the table. Hedda returns to the drawing room. George continues:)*

GEORGE. *(Shocked.)* There you are, Judge! Withdrawn — you see?

BRACK. So yet another honour is about to descend on you.

GEORGE. I'm struck dumb!

BRACK. Congratulations. Of course you're pleased.

GEORGE. I am — I am — I am — I am! Thank you so much! Very kind of you, Judge! You're much, much too generous.

HEDDA. Are you alright?

GEORGE. I'm stunned! Flabbergasted! Oh my goodness …

BRACK. In our small group, Hedda, a success for one is a success for all.

HEDDA. *(Quickly.)* I've cold punch in there. Who's for a glass?

BRACK. Splendid. Professor?

GEORGE. Yes! By God, yes, indeed yes!

HEDDA. Mr. Loevborg?

LOEVBORG. Not for me, thank you.

BRACK. Only cold punch, man. It's not poison.

LOEVBORG. Not for you maybe.

HEDDA. You two go inside. I'll entertain Mr. Loevborg here.

GEORGE. Do that, Hedda. Eilert Loevborg is a major artist and a very, very great man. *(Brack and Tesman go into the back room where they drink and chat and smoke. Hedda picks up a photograph album from the writing desk.)*

HEDDA. Could you endure this? — holiday photographs. I know — guaranteed to bore.

LOEVBORG. I'd love to see them.

HEDDA. Worse — honeymoon photographs — the ultimate boredom. *(She sits in a corner of the couch. He stands looking down at her. Then he takes a chair beside her, his back to the other room. Hedda is a little uneasy and speaks more loudly than necessary.)* Mostly of the Tyrol. You've never been there? Exciting forests, exciting food, exciting people; and their magnificent peasant costumes. And these are the Ortler Mountains. See? — George has written the name so carefully underneath: "O-r-t-l-"

LOEVBORG. Hedda — Gabler.

HEDDA. Shhh.

LOEVBORG. Hedda — Gabler.

HEDDA. That used to be my name. Not now.

LOEVBORG. Can I never say Hedda Gabler again?

HEDDA. I'm not Hedda Gabler any longer.

LOEVBORG. Yes, you're Hedda Tesman now. For God's sake how could you?

HEDDA. Stop it at once! *(George approaches.)* And this is the Ampezzo valley. And those mountains — they're a bit hazy — they're — what's the name of that range, George?

GEORGE. Let me see.

HEDDA. You're slipping. No careful name written at the bottom.

GEORGE. The Dolomites.

HEDDA. Of course — the Dolomites.

GEORGE. A glass of punch, Hedda?

HEDDA. Please. And some canapés.

GEORGE. A cigarette?

HEDDA. Not just now.

GEORGE. Certainly, madam. *(George returns to Brack. Every so often Brack looks sharply at Hedda and Loevborg.)*

LOEVBORG. For God's sake how could you, Hedda?

HEDDA. And that's the Dolomites again from the other side of the valley.

LOEVBORG. Answer me, Hedda.

HEDDA. If you keep calling me Hedda, I won't talk to you at all.

LOEVBORG. Not even when we're alone?

HEDDA. Think it if you want but don't say it.

LOEVBORG. Because you love George Tesman?

HEDDA. Now you're being ridiculous.

LOEVBORG. Don't you love him?

HEDDA. I will not be unfaithful. Is that understood?

LOEVBORG. Then tell me this, Hedda: why did you — ?

HEDDA. Shhh. *(George returns with a tray, glasses, canapés.)*

GEORGE. Not only is he a highly regarded doctor and a professor of great distinction but he is also a waiter of skill and grace. *(Bows to Hedda.)* Madam.

HEDDA. Bertha would have done that.

GEORGE. It pleases me to serve you.

HEDDA. Why the two glasses? Mr. Loevborg isn't drinking.

GEORGE. One for you. One for Mrs. Elvsted.

HEDDA. *(Remembering.)* Ah. Just leave it there.

GEORGE. Had you forgotten the woman dedicated to her anxieties? *(To Loevborg.)* One of the Judge's little drolleries.

HEDDA. Can't you read your writing, George. What's the name of that village?

GEORGE. Yes — it's called — at the foot of the Bremner Pass — can't read it either — it's called — Gone! We spent a night there, remember?

HEDDA. And those three engineers who attached themselves to us after dinner.

GEORGE. The three Spaniards! How could I forget? They couldn't take their eyes off her all night.

HEDDA. Nonsense.

GEORGE. You should have been there, Eilert. *(He joins Judge Brack again.)*

LOEVBORG. Just tell me one thing, Hedda —

HEDDA. He's wrong. They were Italian.

LOEVBORG. You did love me, didn't you? Even a little? Even a passing flutter?

HEDDA. Did I? I don't know. We were close friends — I do know that. *(Smiling.)* All those secrets you told me — you held nothing back. You told me absolutely everything. Maybe that created the illusion of love.

LOEVBORG. You had to hear everything.

HEDDA. Of course. And at the same time I thought: how courageous of him to be so open. Have you any idea how thrilling it all was for me?

LOEVBORG. We sat on the sofa in the drawing room; the general over at the window with his back to us, reading the newspaper — remember? And we pretended to be engrossed in a magazine — always the same one.

HEDDA. We needed a fascinating honeymoon album.

LOEVBORG. *(Now very softly.)* And I told you things about myself — whispered things that nobody in the world had ever heard. Tales of months lost in an alcoholic fog. Weeks of willful degradation. Crude, debauched, driven nights. You burrowed into me. You were able to winkle out even the most minute details as if you had some power over me.

HEDDA. Had I?

LOEVBORG. And those sly questions of yours; never direct; always oblique.

HEDDA. But you understood them perfectly.

LOEVBORG. Of course I did. But sometimes, when you kept burrowing, insisting on more and more exact detail, I sometimes thought — I used to wonder — how could such a young and sheltered girl, a green child really, how could she be so ... without shame.

HEDDA. My recollection is that you were eager to provide every exact detail, Mr. Loevborg.

LOEVBORG. We seemed to be altogether alone in the world, isolated in a kind of hothouse intimacy. But wasn't that a sort of love, too? Because when I confessed everything to you, didn't you want to take me in your arms and absolve me and wash me clean? There must have been a kind of love in that, wasn't there?

HEDDA. *(Dismissively.)* Nothing at all to do with love.

LOEVBORG. Why the relentless interrogation then — that ravenous burrowing? Why? *(Hedda responds slowly and with consideration.)*

HEDDA. I was a young girl, an only child. Yes, a green child. I lived with a widowed father in draughty quarters in the centre of an army barrack. I had no relations, no friends, no companions. I knew that on the other side of the barrack wall people were living joyous and exciting lives. And because that life was far beyond my reach, I had to have it. And you were my guide around that world because you had experienced it in every extreme. I relished that experience through you, my surrogate out there. All those things I was ravenous to learn, that no one had any suspicion I was hearing, that no green girl ought to hear, I heard it all from you, my mentor. You were my tutor in all the delights and excesses and squalor I might never have known. And I experienced them all through you — in blushing secrecy, in absolute safety.

LOEVBORG. But we *were* such friends, Hedda. That friendship should have survived.

HEDDA. That was your fault.

LOEVBORG. You broke it off.

HEDDA. Because you wanted to move it on to a different plane. You misread me, Eilert; I wasn't really without shame. To be shameless required audacity. So I convinced myself that that hothouse intimacy was sufficient for me. And your sudden change — your new demands — terrified me.

LOEVBORG. Then why didn't you shoot me when you threatened

to? Your father's pistol was still on the table.

HEDDA. Cowardice.

LOEVBORG. Yes, you are a coward.

HEDDA. Terrified of scandal.

LOEVBORG. Maybe surrogate living is all you're capable of.

HEDDA. So you fled up to Trondheim where the Elvsteds consoled you.

LOEVBORG. I can imagine what Thea has told you.

HEDDA. Not a word. Have you told Thea about you and me?

LOEVBORG. She wouldn't understand. She's a fool.

HEDDA. Thea's not a fool.

LOEVBORG. Well, foolish about complex things like that. *(Hedda leans closer to him. Her eyes are on the ground. She speaks softly.)*

HEDDA. I have something to tell you, Eilert. Not picking up my father's pistol — that wasn't my greatest cowardice that night. A leap with you had to be made; it was time for it. A huge leap for me. And I wanted so much to make it — I can't tell you — so much, so much. But I just couldn't find the courage to take that leap with you.

LOEVBORG. I knew that at the time. You had a surfeit of my reports, of a mediated life. You wanted immediate life. *(He catches her hand.)* Yes, I knew that then. It's true now too. *(She withdraws her hand very quickly.)*

HEDDA. Careful — that'll do — that's enough — too much. *(Bertha enters with Mrs. Elvsted. Hedda puts the album away, jumps to her feet and flashes a smile. Bertha exits immediately.)* Thea! Come in — come in! Very, very good to see you again. *(Mrs. Elvsted bows to Brack and George as she passes them. She and Loevborg nod to one another. Hedda grips Thea's hand.)*

THEA. Shouldn't I say a word to Mr. Tesman?

HEDDA. They're happy as they are. And they'll be leaving us soon.

THEA. Where are they going?

HEDDA. Out on the town. Or to use one of Judge Brack's Americanisms — where does he pick them up? — they're going on the razzle-dazzle.

THEA. *(Quickly.)* Not you, Eilert?

HEDDA. Mr. Loevborg is staying here with the prudent women.

THEA. I'm so relaxed — so happy — to be here. *(Thea takes a chair to sit beside Loevborg.)*

HEDDA. No, not there, Thea darling. Sit here *(On the sofa.)* beside me. I must be in the centre of things, mustn't I?

THEA. As you wish, Hedda.

LOEVBORG. *(To Hedda.)* Isn't she lovely to look at?

HEDDA. *(Stroking Thea's hair.)* Just to consider?

LOEVBORG. Just to contemplate. We are soul mates, Thea and I. We have total trust in one another. We can sit and talk with complete openness.

HEDDA. No obliquity?

THEA. *(To Loevborg.)* I've got to tell Hedda what you say.

LOEVBORG. Say about what? *(Pause.)*

HEDDA. Well?

THEA. *(Softly. To Hedda.)* He says I inspire him.

HEDDA. "Oh my goodness." And do you? *(To Loevborg.)* Does she?

LOEVBORG. She's a very courageous woman.

THEA. Not really.

LOEVBORG. When it comes to helping her soul mate, to battling on his behalf, she is altogether without fear.

HEDDA. I envy you. Maybe if I had that sort of courage, then perhaps I could manage the business of life … maybe. *(Sudden change.)* Now, Thea, a glass of cold punch.

THEA. Not for me, thanks. I never touch alcohol.

HEDDA. Mr. Loevborg?

LOEVBORG. Nothing for me either.

THEA. He's fine, Hedda.

LOEVBORG. We're a pair of killjoys.

HEDDA. But if I wanted you to?

LOEVBORG. Why would that make a difference?

HEDDA. So I have no power over you at all?

LOEVBORG. Not in this matter.

HEDDA. Well, I think you should have a glass.

THEA. Hedda!

HEDDA. For your own sake.

LOEVBORG. I don't know what that means.

HEDDA. And to perplex other people —

LOEVBORG. Who?

HEDDA. — who might suspect that in your heart of hearts you aren't as assured as you appear, that you're quite irresolute in fact.

THEA. Oh, Hedda, no!

HEDDA. To confound them.

LOEVBORG. Let them suspect what they like.

THEA. He's right. Who cares about them?

HEDDA. I could see it in the Judge just now, how scornful he was when he saw you were afraid to join them in a drink.

LOEVBORG. I wanted to stay here and talk to you.

HEDDA. "Only cold punch, man. It's not poison." And when you didn't dare go to their stupid party, I saw him winking at George.

LOEVBORG. *(Very controlled.)* I didn't dare?

HEDDA. That's what the shrewd judge thought.

LOEVBORG. *(Shrugs.)* Who cares what he thinks.

HEDDA. So you're not going with them?

LOEVBORG. Haven't I already said I'm staying here with you and Thea?

HEDDA. Good.

LOEVBORG. What's got into you, Hedda?

HEDDA. *(Quickly, sharply.)* What do you mean by that?

LOEVBORG. I don't know what's going on here. I was invited to a dinner party. I said no. I was offered a glass of cold port. I said no. Can I be any more explicit?

HEDDA. You're a man of iron discipline. Altogether admirable. *(She strokes Thea's cheek.)* Thea tells us you're … impeccable.

THEA. *(Confused.)* Hedda, what are you — ?

HEDDA. And she's right. The peccable Eilert that I admired belongs to the past. That's what I tried to tell you this morning. But nothing would convince her you weren't already off on the "razzle-dazzle." As Eilert says, you're a very silly woman.

THEA. *(Shocked.)* Eilert — ? You two were talking about me behind — ?

HEDDA. Consider him, Thea. Is that a man on the verge of collapsing again? You're still not anxious for him, are you?

LOEVBORG. Something *has* got into you.

THEA. Hedda, dear God, Hedda, what are you trying to do?

HEDDA. Keep your voice down. That awful judge is listening.

LOEVBORG. *(To Thea.)* Anxious for me, were you?

THEA. *(About to cry.)* Oh my God …

LOEVBORG. And in panic? Your faith in me is moving. *(To Thea.)* To your great belief in me. *(He picks up a glass and drinks it quickly.)*

THEA. This is what you wanted to happen, isn't it?

LOEVBORG. And to Mrs. Tesman and her ugly manipulations. *(He begins to fill the glass again. Hedda restrains him.)*

HEDDA. That's enough. You've a dinner party to go to.

THEA. He's not going to that, Hedda!

HEDDA. Quiet. You're being watched. *(Loevborg puts the glass down.)*

LOEVBORG. Tell me truthfully, Thea: did your husband know you followed me here?

THEA. Oh, Hedda …

LOEVBORG. Was it agreed between you and the resident magistrate that you would come and spy on me? He wasn't genuinely concerned for his children's tutor, was he? Or did he just want me back to make up his card school?

THEA. *(Now crying.)* Eilert, please, Eilert … *(Loevborg raises the glass again.)*

LOEVBORG. To the resident magistrate and his obedient wife. *(Again Hedda stops him.)*

HEDDA. I've said that's enough. You've promised to read part of your book to George. *(He is suddenly calm and controlled again.)*

LOEVBORG. You're so right. I'm sorry, Thea. Pardon your soul mate. I'm really sorry. No need for anxiety — I'll be fine. Don't panic. Remember: you *have* rescued me. We both believe that. I'll be just fine. Promise.

THEA. I know you will. I trust you totally. *(Brack and George come down to the drawing room.)*

BRACK. Time for us to leave, Mrs. Tesman.

HEDDA. So soon?

BRACK. Dionysus is getting impatient.

LOEVBORG. *(Suddenly.)* Count me in!

THEA. *(In panic.)* Eilert! Eilert Loevborg — !

HEDDA. *(Squeezing her arm.)* Control yourself.

BRACK. *(To Loevborg.)* You know you may be exposing yourself to a minor misconduct?

LOEVBORG. *(Laughs.)* May I, please?

BRACK. *(Quietly to George.)* I did confess my unease with the St. Paul canard, didn't I?

GEORGE. *(Laughs.)* Judge Brack!

BRACK. Not converted. Concussed by the fall from his horse.

LOEVBORG. *(Picking up his manuscript. To George.)* A few chapters I'd like to show you before it goes off to the publisher.

GEORGE. I can't wait. Hold on — how is Mrs. Elvsted to get home?

LOEVBORG. I'll see Mrs. Elvsted home. Who else? About ten o'clock, Mrs. Tesman — will that suit you?

HEDDA. Perfect.

GEORGE. I'm afraid I may not be back by ten, Hedda. What do you think, Judge?

BRACK. A.M. or P.M.?

HEDDA. *(Caution.)* Judge!

BRACK. Depends on how successful we are at razzling-dazzling. Or is it razzle-dazzling? Or razzling-dazzle?

HEDDA. Don't rush home on my account.

GEORGE. Ten o'clock, Eilert?

LOEVBORG. On the dot.

THEA. Promise, Eilert?

BRACK. Never exact a promise. Like the oath in court, nobody trusts it for a second.

HEDDA. I'd give a lot to be a fly on your wall, Judge.

BRACK. Not advisable. You might see things not at all suitable for a mind of such manifest innocence.

GEORGE. Ten o'clock, Thea?

THEA. Please. *(Brack, George and Loevborg all leave. Bertha enters and lights a lamp. She then clears away the glasses.)* What will happen, Hedda?

HEDDA. What will happen is that he will come home — when he comes home — with a wreath of vine leaves in his damp hair; gleaming, triumphant, exuding power.

THEA. He will look after himself, won't he?

HEDDA. He'll be his own master again — a free man again.

THEA. Oh God, I hope he is alright.

HEDDA. I don't doubt him. My faith in the real Eilert Loevborg is absolute. Which of us will be proved right, Thea?

THEA. You're after something, Hedda. What are you after?

HEDDA. *(Brief pause.)* For once in my life I want control over the destiny of a man.

THEA. You already have that power. You have George.

HEDDA. *(Laughs.)* Don't be stupid. Who would want to shape that fate? Don't you appreciate, sweet little Thea, how poor and disadvantaged I am and how opulent and privileged you are? *(She suddenly embraces her.)* There's a whiff of expectancy in the atmosphere. Don't you smell it? I think I'll set fire to your hair after all. *(Thea jumps up.)*

THEA. Let me go! Let go of me! You terrify me, Hedda! *(Bertha enters.)*

BERTHA. I've laid the tea things in the dining room.

HEDDA. Good. We're coming.

THEA. I'm going home, Hedda — now — by myself. Sorry. I can't stay here. I'm too scared of —

HEDDA. Oh shut up, you fool! You're going to have supper first with terrifying Hedda. And then — then Eilert Loevborg will come. With a crown of vine leaves in his damp hair. *(Quick black.)*

End of Act Two

ACT THREE

Dawn the following day. The curtains are closed. The lamp is turned low and still burning.

Hedda, fully dressed, is asleep on the sofa. She is covered by a rug. Thea is in an armchair beside the stove, her feet on a stool, a large shawl around her shoulders.

A noise offstage. Thea sits up suddenly and listens intensely, then sinks back again.

THEA.   Oh my God, no ... *(Bertha enters on tiptoe.)* What was that?

BERTHA.   A girl came with this letter.

THEA.   *(Holds out her hand.)* Thank you, Bertha.

BERTHA.   It's for Dr. Tesman, ma'am.

THEA.   Ah.

BERTHA.   From his aunt, Miss Juliana. That big rough lump of a maid of hers brought it. I'll leave it here *(Table.)* for him. Better put that lamp out. Beginning to smoke.

THEA.   It'll soon be daylight.

BERTHA.   It's daylight already, ma'am. *(She turns the lamp off.)*

THEA.   Still no sign of the men?

BERTHA.   You might have known. Once they fell in with that certain gentleman there was bound to be bother. We all know his pedigree.

THEA.   You'll waken Mrs. Tesman.

BERTHA.   Will I put some wood on the stove?

THEA.   Not for me, thank you. The room's quite warm. *(Bertha exits. The noise wakens Hedda.)*

HEDDA.   What's that?

THEA.   Bertha, the maid.

HEDDA.   *(Stretching.)* What time is it, Thea?

THEA.   After seven.

HEDDA. When did George get home?

THEA. He's not back yet. Nobody's back yet.

HEDDA. And we sat up like fools till four!

THEA. You had a good sleep.

HEDDA. I had. And you?

THEA. Not a wink.

HEDDA. Didn't even doze?

THEA. I had a miserable night. *(Hedda goes to her.)*

HEDDA. I know … I know … But there is nothing to worry about. I know only too well what happened.

THEA. What?

HEDDA. They had a very heavy night at the judge's.

THEA. *(Anxiously.)* Did they?

HEDDA. It's always much worse than they expect. And George didn't dare face in here in that condition in the middle of the night. So off he went to the aunts — they keep his old room for him.

THEA. No, he's not there. A letter came from there just now.

HEDDA. *(Picks up the letter.)* Ah — Aunt Juliana's handwriting. Then he's still at Judge Brack's.

THEA. You know very well they're not still at the judge's home, Hedda.

HEDDA. Thea, darling, you look completely washed out.

THEA. I am.

HEDDA. Then go upstairs to my bedroom and lie down. First on the right at the top of the stairs. A sleep will restore you.

THEA. I couldn't sleep, Hedda. I'll wait until George comes back and he'll know where —

HEDDA. I'll call you the moment he comes. There is no point in sitting up here — now is there?

THEA. You're right, I suppose.

HEDDA. You *will* sleep.

THEA. And you'll call me?

HEDDA. Promise.

THEA. For a short while then. *(Thea exits. Hedda pulls back the curtains and the room is flooded with morning sunshine. She takes a hand mirror from the drawer of the desk, examines her face, deftly arranges her hair. Then she rings the bell for Bertha. Bertha enters.)*

HEDDA. You let the fire die. The room's freezing.

BERTHA. I offered to —

HEDDA. Put some logs on now.

BERTHA. Yes, ma'am. *(The doorbell rings.)*

HEDDA. Answer that. I'll look after the stove. *(Hedda kneels in front of the stove. George enters. He tries to tiptoe soundlessly up to the back room. Not looking up:)* Good morning.

GEORGE. *(Loud and breezy.)* Hedda! Good morning to you, too. You're up early. I thought you'd still be asleep.

HEDDA. No need to shout. Mrs. Elvsted's up in my bed.

GEORGE. She spent the night here?

HEDDA. None of you gentlemen remembered to take her home, did you?

GEORGE. I know. Sorry about that. The thought did come into my head a few times during the night, but between one thing and another … *(Hedda closes the door of the stove and stands up.)*

HEDDA. Well, had you a good time?

GEORGE. Were you worried about me?

HEDDA. I asked had you a good time.

GEORGE. Yes. I suppose so. The usual. *(Laughs.)* At one point in the night the judge announced he was getting too old for "making whoopee." He says that's a Navaho Indian expression.

HEDDA. Did Eilert Loevborg behave himself?

GEORGE. For a full hour he read to me from his new book. In the judge's breakfast room. Just the two of us alone there together. I was mesmerised, Hedda. For a full hour. *(Hedda sits at the table.)*

HEDDA. Well, aren't you going to tell me about it? *(Pause.)*

GEORGE. It is just amazing, Hedda. Eilert Loevborg has written an amazing book. What can I tell you? Utterly amazing.

HEDDA. *(Coldly.)* So Mr. Loevborg's book amazed you.

GEORGE. Probably the most remarkable book I've ever read! The clarity, the insights, the poise — I can't think of any book that had such a profound impact on me.

HEDDA. "Oh my goodness."

GEORGE. And as I listened to him reading, Hedda, I must confess I had the strangest experience. I was astounded by the book — of course, of course I was; overawed by it. But at the same time a portion of me stayed very cool and very analytical. And I suddenly knew I was jealous of Eilert Loevborg. I thought: it's a bit unfair, isn't it, that a man so weak and so damaged should have been endowed with this enormous talent? He doesn't value it. He has no real interest in it. He's not capable of protecting and nurturing it. That's a little unfair, isn't it?

HEDDA. Is it?

GEORGE. It is. Because for all his genius he just can't cope.

HEDDA. Cope with what? Mediocrity? The second-rate?

GEORGE. Just with being alive, I suppose. Maybe just … living is beyond him.

HEDDA. Many people have that problem. That doesn't mean he's damaged. Anyhow, how did the night end?

GEORGE. I'm afraid the night just … disintegrated. Dionysian, I'm sorry to say.

HEDDA. Did he have vine leaves in his hair?

GEORGE. *(Puzzled.)* Eilert? No, I don't recall vine leaves. No, he was wearing a tweed cap. Yes, a brown tweed cap. I remember him holding it against his chest when he delivered this long oration about the splendid woman who inspired him to write the book.

HEDDA. Thea?

GEORGE. Addicted-to-her-anxieties Thea, as the judge calls her. He didn't name her, but we all knew who he meant. And that was the word he used, Hedda — "inspired"!

HEDDA. Drunken blether. When did you break up?

GEORGE. I've no idea what time it was. We all left the judge's place together. Brack came some of the way with us — to clear his head. Poor old Eilert was in bits: we almost had to carry him.

HEDDA. *(Ironically.)* Never!

GEORGE. And then a strange thing happened. No, not a strange thing; a very funny thing. No, not a funny thing at all; actually a tragic thing. No, no, that's too strong. A sad thing, yes; yes, a very sad thing happened.

HEDDA. *(Exaggerated patience.)* What happened, George?

GEORGE. The others were in front of me. I had fallen a little behind. I ran to catch up with them. And what do you think I found lying at the side of the road?

HEDDA. *(Crossly.)* Please.

GEORGE. You mustn't tell a soul, Hedda; for Eilert's sake. Promise me that. *(He produces a large envelope from the pocket of his overcoat — the manuscript.)*

HEDDA. Not the "amazing" new book?

GEORGE. Yes.

HEDDA. The one he read to you for an hour last night?

GEORGE. Yes.

HEDDA. The manuscript he had here yesterday?

GEORGE. Yes.

HEDDA. He wasn't aware he had lost it?

GEORGE. No.

HEDDA. Why didn't you give it back to him there and then?

GEORGE. In the state he was in!

HEDDA. You didn't tell any of the others?

GEORGE. I felt I oughtn't to — for Eilert's sake.

HEDDA. So nobody knows you have it?

GEORGE. And nobody's going to know. I'll give it to him later today when he has sobered up.

HEDDA. How was he when you saw him last?

GEORGE. Almost footless. In the centre of town. But determined not to let the night end. That's when we all broke up. The judge disappeared somewhere. A couple of us bribed a night watchman to share his poisonous coffee with us. Two others went off some-where with Eilert: they told me they were bringing him home but they were going in the wrong direction! All very messy. I'm feeling a little fragile — would you mind if I lay down for an hour? Then I'll go to Eilert's. *(He picks up the manuscript.)*

HEDDA. Let me read it first.

GEORGE. Oh, Hedda, you couldn't do that.

HEDDA. Couldn't or daren't?

GEORGE. Wouldn't it be a little ... intrusive? I mean it's very per-sonal to him; like a diary. And when he wakes up and finds it gone, can you imagine the panic he'll be in?

HEDDA. He can rewrite it, can't he?

GEORGE. I wouldn't think so. Something as unique as that can be produced only under a great urgency of inspiration. Wouldn't you agree?

HEDDA. I wouldn't know. I'm not a great writer like you people. By the way — a letter for you. *(He examines the envelope.)*

GEORGE. Auntie Juju's writing. *(He leaves the manuscript on the stool and sits to read the letter.)* I love her handwriting; it's so resolute ... Oh my God, Hedda, Auntie Rena's dying! Oh my God!

HEDDA. You expected that, didn't you?

GEORGE. I'm to go at once if I hope to see her. Of course I do! Of course I will! Poor, poor Auntie Rena. I never expected this — not really. I'll go straight away. Come with me, Hedda, will you, please?

HEDDA. No, no, don't ask that of me.

GEORGE. But Hedda love —

HEDDA. Please, George.

GEORGE. You won't have a chance to see her again.

HEDDA. I couldn't face it. I couldn't look at her. Don't ask that of me, George. No, no, I can't look at anything at all like that. Please.

GEORGE. I see ... *(Sudden panic.)* Where's my coat? My hat? In the hall! Don't need gloves, do I? — it's September, isn't it? — I hope I'll make it in time. *(Bertha enters.)*

BERTHA. Excuse me, Doctor —

GEORGE. Auntie Rena's dying, Bertha.

BERTHA. Oh Mother of God!

GEORGE. Our lovely Auntie Rena's slipping away.

BERTHA. Mother of God, my lovely Miss Rena.

GEORGE. I'm on my way over. I'll bring her your love.

BERTHA. Yes, yes, Georgie! All my love! Mother of God, my lovely Miss Rena — oh sweet Mother of God. *(Bertha begins to cry.)*

HEDDA. What is it you want?

BERTHA. What's that?

HEDDA. Do you want something?

BERTHA. Judge Brack is here.

GEORGE. What the hell's Brack doing here at this moment? I can't see him now.

HEDDA. I can. Tell him to come in. *(As Bertha leaves, sobbing, George goes to her and catches her elbow.)*

GEORGE. I know. Thank you, Bertha. I know. Our lovely Miss Rena. Thank you. *(To Hedda.)* I'll slip out this way.

HEDDA. The manuscript, George.

GEORGE. Yes, give it to me.

HEDDA. Why would you take it to your aunts? I'll look after it here.

GEORGE. You're right. Of course. Good. I'm off. *(He exits. Hedda places the manuscript in the bookcase above the desk. Brack enters.)*

BRACK. I know — I know — an unconscionable hour again. It's becoming a sad little habit. Why can't I discipline myself to stay away?

HEDDA. You just missed George. His Aunt Rena is dying.

BRACK. Ah, melancholy tidings. Such honourable girls, those Tesman ladies. George will be perturbed.

HEDDA. Probably. I gather last night's party was ... robust?

BRACK. Is that the verdict? Verging on the turbulent, I'd suggest. *(He opens his coat.)* Haven't had time to change — that's the telltale. Did Tesman enjoy himself?

56

HEDDA. What did he tell me? Eilert Loevborg declared that his new book was "inspired" by the anxious Thea?

BRACK. He did indeed — solemnly.

HEDDA. Judge Brack declared he is getting too old for "making whoopee"

BRACK. He did indeed — jestingly. Do you know what making whoopee means?

HEDDA. No.

BRACK. I tell myself it's an American-Indian word for making love. And if it is, I'm not too old at all. In fact, elegant Hedda, I'm only approaching my peak.

HEDDA. *(Laughs.)* And George and two others cadged bad coffee from a night watchman.

BRACK. Loevborg wasn't one of the two?

HEDDA. No. George thought Loevborg had gone home at that stage.

BRACK. Decent, credulous, trusting George. That's what they wanted him to believe. Have you any idea where Loevborg and his two friends spent the residue of the night?

HEDDA. Why do I expect somewhere improper?

BRACK. Because you're a very naughty woman, thank heavens. And you're so right. I knew Loevborg had got an invitation earlier in the day. But he declined because — as we all assumed — he is ... "delivered"?

HEDDA. Saved, Judge. *(Brack crosses his arms in front of his face to ward off evil — as he did before.)*

BRACK. Please! So he resisted the invite with valiance until alcohol undermined him, and himself and the others ended up in the establishment of a Mademoiselle Circe.

HEDDA. Circe?

BRACK. A pseudonym. Yes, a little flamboyant. But then she is a lady with classical inclinations as well.

HEDDA. A sort of singer-dancer?

BRACK. Among other accomplishments.

HEDDA. Red-haired?

BRACK. You've heard of her then?

HEDDA. She carries a revolver in her handbag.

BRACK. That I didn't know. So you and she share a passion for artillery? Yes, some years ago Mademoiselle Circe was up before me on some charge or other. In those days her more decorous name was Mary Bridget O'Donnell. Eilert Loevborg was a client of hers back then, too. *(Trying to remember.)* What was the charge? Yes, cruelty to animals. Surely there's no connection between that and her profession?

HEDDA. And last night ended badly?

BRACK. And it began with amity and protestations of affection. Ended very badly indeed. Loevborg accused Circe of larceny. Circe replied with a smackeroo on the kisser: smackeroo — thump; kisser — *(He points to his mouth.)*

HEDDA. What had she stolen?

BRACK. Both Americanisms. Stolen? — his wallet, some coins, and some other important possessions — or so he insists. There was an exchange of blows — yes, male and female. And blood was drawn. Sordid. Anyhow Loevborg was arrested and removed to the police station where he was most truculent: lacerated a young officer's uniform and then rendered him horizontal. The police are my source of all this squalid information. As I say sometimes when I'm on the bench and wish to sound impressively judicial, I say: how can civilised people sink so low?

HEDDA. So there were no vine leaves in his hair?

BRACK. No. Not mentioned in the police report. They know, of course, that he spent the early part of the evening at my house. That could be embarrassing for me.

HEDDA. He'll be up in court then?

BRACK. Probably. And you could well be caught up in the embarrassment.

HEDDA. How?

BRACK. He is a guest here. As we talk, his "inspiration" sleeps upstairs, Bertha tells me. And Mrs. Elvsted won't be returning to the resident magistrate in the near future.

HEDDA. There are many places she and Loevborg can meet.

BRACK. No respectable house in this city will welcome them from now on.

HEDDA. Including this respectable house?

BRACK. I would hope so. I would be quite displeased if Eilert Loevborg were welcome here. If I were to discover that he was intruding —

HEDDA. On the triangle?

BRACK. That would be like losing a home.

HEDDA. You want to be the only rooster in the yard?

BRACK. Of course. And I shall fight for that in every way I know how, lovely Hedda; every way.

HEDDA. *(Uneasily.)* You are a dangerous man, Judge Brack.

BRACK. *(Pretended hurt.)* I'm not — am I?

HEDDA. Thank goodness you haven't any kind of hold over me.

BRACK. No, not now.

HEDDA. Do I detect a threat there?

BRACK. Hedda! The triangle can flourish only with mutual consent. Compulsion would poison the benign atmosphere. And now I must depart. And please do something about a crack in the door of your bedroom: you know how I adore contemplating you.

HEDDA. You're going out through the garden?

BRACK. Shorter, isn't it?

HEDDA. And devious.

BRACK. You mean devious as in *de via,* off the main track, don't you?

HEDDA. Do I?

BRACK. I think so. A woman like you knows that following an erratic course can be exciting.

HEDDA. So can firing a pistol.

BRACK. *(Laughs.)* Thank heavens people don't shoot tame roosters.

HEDDA. Especially when they've got only one. *(They both laugh as he exits. She shuts the French windows behind him and watches him as he leaves. Then she goes to the desk and takes the manuscript from the bookcase. She begins to read it but stops when she hears raised voices in the hall. She listens for a few seconds, puts the manuscript in the drawer of the desk and locks it.)*

BERTHA. *(Offstage.)* You're not going in there, sir!

LOEVBORG. *(Offstage.)* Out of my way, woman!

BERTHA. *(Offstage.)* Take your dirty hands off me!

LOEVBORG. *(Offstage.)* I am going in! Out of my way! Let me pass! *(The door is flung open. Loevborg bursts in. His hair is wild, his clothes disheveled and he has a small plaster on his lip. When he sees Hedda he makes an effort to control himself — and bows to her.)*

HEDDA. So Mr. Loevborg has finally turned up. A little late to take Thea home, isn't it?

LOEVBORG. I know. I'm sorry. And forgive this ... *(Appearance.)*

HEDDA. How did you know she's still here?

LOEVBORG. I went to her lodging. They said she hadn't returned.

HEDDA. And were they surprised?

LOEVBORG. At what?

HEDDA. Didn't they think it strange that you called?

LOEVBORG. That this disheveled creature was looking for her? If they did, they gave no indication. George isn't up yet?

HEDDA. Not yet.

LOEVBORG. When did he get home?

HEDDA. Very late.

LOEVBORG. What did he tell you about last night?

HEDDA. It was the usual disgraceful affair at the judge's.

LOEVBORG. Nothing else?

HEDDA. I don't remember. I was half asleep. *(Thea Elvsted runs in from the back room and goes straight to Loevborg. She catches both his hands in hers and her eyes search his face anxiously.)*

THEA. Eilert! Oh Eilert! At last! Give me your hands! What happened to your face? The patient hands are so cold. Is your jacket torn? You're very pale, Eilert — are you alright?

LOEVBORG. Too late, Thea. Finished.

THEA. Too late? What's too late? What's finished?

LOEVBORG. I'm washed up. It's all over. I've come to the end.

THEA. I will not listen to —

LOEVBORG. When you've heard what happened last night you'll —

THEA. I don't care what happened last night. Last night's over. We've had these setbacks before and we struggled through and triumphed.

HEDDA. I'll leave you two alone.

LOEVBORG. No, stay, please.

THEA. Today is a new day, Eilert. Today you'll make a fresh beginning.

LOEVBORG. I'm not talking about last night's party. I'm talking about you and me, Thea. We're finished, too.

THEA. Finished? Eilert, we —

LOEVBORG. We mustn't see each other again.

THEA. Hedda, tell him to —

LOEVBORG. I don't need you anymore. I don't mean to sound so brutal. But the working partnership we had is finished.

THEA. You're upset, Eilert. Something happened last night that —

LOEVBORG. Listen to what I'm saying to you. I'm never going to write ever again. My life is over. All done with. So is our work together, our working partnership — that's over, too.

THEA. But we're collaborators, Eilert, soul mates —

LOEVBORG. Finished. Completely finished. So what you must do is expel me and all that past from your head — completely.

THEA. He doesn't mean it, Hedda?

LOEVBORG. And begin to assemble a new life for yourself.

THEA. That's not possible.

LOEVBORG. You're a young woman, you're very competent, everything is still very possible for you. Go back to Trondheim and your family and —

THEA. Never that! Can't do that! Oh Eilert! I don't believe that that's all it was to you — a working partnership. I know it was much, much richer than that. I know it was. Have you any idea what you're doing to me? You can't discard me like that. You are my life, Eilert; the only life I have. I don't exist unless I'm with you. You *do* know that, don't you? And I have got to be with you when the new book comes out, Eilert, our book, yours and mine. I do have that right. Because it is ours, Eilert. We are its parents.

LOEVBORG. We were.

THEA. And I have got to witness the happiness on your face, and the delight and satisfaction of hearing people applaud you and praise you and lay before you all the honour and respect you have always deserved. Because it will be an occasion of such joy for us, Eilert. Yes, of course it will be a literary event too — "significant" and "groundbreaking." But for us — for you and for me — it will be just so joyous, just so happy, just such a private and intense celebration. Oh Eilert, I have got to be there to share that happiness with you. Even just to witness it. And to see that old Eilert Loevborg — that damaged, hesitant, apologetic, irresolute, flinching Eilert Loevborg — to have him exorcised forever. You can understand that, can't you?

LOEVBORG. There won't be a book launch, Thea. There can't be a book launch. There is no book.

THEA. I don't understand what —

LOEVBORG. There is no longer a book to launch.

THEA. Of course there is a book, Eilert. We laboured over it for eighteen months. And when we were finished, I wrote out the entire manuscript myself in my own hand.

LOEVBORG. That manuscript is torn up, Thea.

THEA. Torn up?

LOEVBORG. I destroyed that manuscript; tore it up; into shreds.

THEA. But Eilert —

LOEVBORG. That manuscript doesn't exist anymore.

THEA. *(Now accepting — and stunned.)* Oh no, noooo …

HEDDA. *(Involuntarily.)* But that's not —

LOEVBORG. Not true, you think?

HEDDA. If you say it is …

LOEVBORG. I've destroyed my life. Why not my work?

THEA. Why would he want to hurt me, Hedda? Tell me it's a lie, Hedda, isn't it?

LOEVBORG. I ripped it into a thousand pieces and threw them into the fjord. They floated for a short time and then sank — just like myself.

THEA. It's the truth, Hedda. He's telling us the awful truth.

HEDDA. Yes.

THEA. You have torn up a life, Eilert. You know that?

LOEVBORG. I know that.

THEA. Destroyed a life I helped to create.

LOEVBORG. Yes.

THEA. Destroyed our child, Eilert Loevborg — you know that. And part of me will be mourning for the rest of my days.

HEDDA. Maybe you should —

THEA. I think I will go now, Hedda.

HEDDA. Back to your lodging?

THEA. My coat and hat are probably on the hall stand. To my lodging? No, not there; not back to Trondheim. No idea where I'm going, Hedda. No idea at all. I think I'll just wander … until the earth goes still again. *(She exits. We hear the front door shut. Pause.)*

HEDDA. Aren't you going to take her to her lodging?

LOEVBORG. She's better not seen with me.

HEDDA. Can't you see she's shattered, Eilert?

LOEVBORG. For a time. Never underestimate Mrs. Elvsted: she's a resilient woman.

HEDDA. What happened last night that was so irrevocable?

LOEVBORG. Oh, I began all over again last night: back to the old treadmill, Hedda. The drinking. The whoring. The brawling. And the curse of it is that I don't have the stomach for it now. Even as I crave it and find satisfaction, it nauseates me. That can end in only one way. In the old days I spat in the face of the world with such easy defiance. So in that she certainly succeeded: she broke my courage; she fractured my will.

HEDDA. *(As though to herself.)* Silly little bitch. Yet somehow she has shaped a man's destiny. *(To Loevborg.)* You were brutal to her, Eilert.

LOEVBORG. She had to look at what had happened.

HEDDA. A part of her *will* be in mourning for the rest of her days.

LOEVBORG. For God's sake! For all of a week — maybe!

HEDDA. To destroy the one thing in her life that she believed made that life cohere — isn't that cruel?

LOEVBORG. I will tell you the truth, Hedda.

HEDDA. About what?

LOEVBORG. Promise me you won't breathe a word of this to Thea.

HEDDA. What are you talking about?

LOEVBORG. The manuscript. Promise.

HEDDA. Promise — promise.

LOEVBORG. I didn't tear it up and throw the pieces in the fjord. But I did defile it.

HEDDA. I don't understand what —

LOEVBORG. Sullied it — contaminated it — betrayed it.

HEDDA. But you still have it.

LOEVBORG. Thea said it was like killing our child. But there are other obscene things a father may do to his child that may be just as evil. Suppose a man comes home in the early hours of the morning and says to the mother of his child, "I have been out brawling and drinking and whoring all night long. And I had our child with me in all of those dens. He watched the brawling and the drinking and he witnessed the whoring. And now our child is lost. I can't find him. I don't know what hands he has fallen into or where they are holding him or what those hands are doing to him."

HEDDA. It's not a child, Eilert. It's a book — a book.

LOEVBORG. Thea's soul was in that book.

HEDDA. I know all that but —

LOEVBORG. She made it her whole life. That book was the repository of all her hopes and aspirations. It was her pure heart that gave that book its shape and quickened it. How can I look into her pure face ever again? I can't — can I? *(Pause.)*

HEDDA. Where will you go?

LOEVBORG. That doesn't matter now. *(Pause.)* Put an end to the whole squalid business.

HEDDA. You mean that?

LOEVBORG. Yes.

HEDDA. You've made your mind up?

LOEVBORG. Yes.

HEDDA. When?

LOEVBORG. *(Shrugs.)* Soon.

HEDDA. Listen to me, Eilert Loevborg. If you do it, when you do it, do it as beautifully as you can.

LOEVBORG. *(Smiles.)* Beautifully? You mean with vine leaves in my hair?

HEDDA. *(Slowly. With deliberation.)* No, none of that nonsense anymore. But with beauty. One beautiful gesture, Eilert Loevborg — a gesture that becomes you. Please. *(Pause.)* And now you must go. Don't come back here again. Goodbye, Eilert Loevborg.

LOEVBORG. Adieu, Hedda Gabler. Give George Tesman my best wishes. *(He turns to go.)*

HEDDA. Wait. A souvenir to take with you. *(She unlocks the desk where she has the manuscript. She takes out the pistol case. She removes one of the pistols and hands it to him.)*

LOEVBORG. This is my souvenir?

HEDDA. Don't you recognise it? I aimed it at you once long ago.

LOEVBORG. You should have used it then.

HEDDA. It might be useful now. *(Hedda takes it and puts it in his breast pocket.)*

LOEVBORG. Thank you.

HEDDA. *(As he leaves.)* And with beauty, Eilert Loevborg. Give me that promise. One beautiful, final gesture. A final gesture that becomes you. *(She goes to the drawer again and takes out the manuscript. She goes to the armchair beside the stove. She sits there with the manuscript on her lap. Now she opens the envelope, pulls out some pages and looks at them. Now she opens the door of the stove and slowly feeds the pages into the flames. As she does:)* This is your child I'm burning, Thea; anxious Thea, Thea with ridiculous golden curls. I'm burning the child you had by him. I'm burning your baby, Thea, your and Eilert Loevborg's baby. *(Fade to black.)*

End of Act Three

ACT FOUR

That same night. The drawing room is in darkness. The back room is lit by a lamp hanging above the table. The curtains are pulled across the French windows. Hedda, dressed in black, paces restlessly round the drawing room. Now she goes up to the back room and plays a few rapid chords on the piano. Now she returns to the drawing room and to her pacing.

Bertha enters with a lighted lamp. She has been crying and has black ribbons in her cap. She places the lamp on the drawing room table.

HEDDA. That lamp is dangerous. Turn the wick down. *(Pause.)* What's your name again?
BERTHA. Bertha.
HEDDA. That wick's too high. *(Pause.)* I'm talking to you, Berna.
BERTHA. I hear you.
HEDDA. That wick is dangerous. Turn it down. *(Bertha does not obey her. She stares at Hedda for a few seconds —a mixture of grief and sullenness and defiance — and shuffles off. To herself:)* Sullen bitch. *(Juliana, dressed in mourning clothes, enters. Hedda goes to her with her hands outstretched.)*
JULIANA. She's gone, Hedda. It's all over.
HEDDA. I know.
JULIANA. Our lovely Rena has left us.
HEDDA. George sent me a quick note.
JULIANA. He said he would but I thought I must tell Hedda myself.
HEDDA. Thank you.
JULIANA. She went so quickly in the end. I just wish she could have chosen a different time to leave us. Hedda's home is a house of happy expectation just now. It shouldn't be overcast by death.
HEDDA. And it was a peaceful end?
JULIANA. Very peaceful. And after a life of suffering borne with such fortitude, that was becoming, wasn't it? She kissed me; and

she kissed Georgie; and she said she was sorry she would miss a new birthday blossom on his slippers next month — she had planned to do a Flower of Bethlehem. Then she asked was Bertha not there and she sent her her special love. Then she sighed once — a mere hint of impatience; just once. And she was gone. It was very beautiful. *(Suddenly brisk.)* He's not home yet?

HEDDA. He said he might be delayed. Take a seat, Miss Tesman.

JULIANA. Thank you, Hedda dear, but I must run. I have to call on the undertaker. And I must do her hair myself: I want her to look really beautiful. She was quite vain about her hair, little Miss Rena, when she was young; such a mass of curls.

HEDDA. Can I help in any way?

JULIANA. I wouldn't hear of it. We can't have Hedda Tesman turning her hand to that kind of work: her thoughts are on happier events, thank goodness. I really must go, Hedda. I still have to sew up Rena's shroud. But it won't be long until there'll be joyous sewing to be done for this house, will it? *(Whispers.)* Aren't you thrilled? I can't wait. *(George enters from the hall. He seems disoriented.)*

HEDDA. *(Sharply.)* You took your time.

GEORGE. Sorry — sorry. Auntie Juju, hello! Didn't know you were here. Did you tell me you were coming? Sorry — I'm a little confused.

JULIANA. Did you get all those messages done?

GEORGE. Most of them. I couldn't remember some of them. Could you write them down for me? *(Juliana catches his elbow.)*

JULIANA. I understand of course, Georgie.

GEORGE. The old head's just a bit addled today.

JULIANA. I know. It's all very sad. But it's a relief, too. You mustn't go under. There are so many arrangements to be made.

GEORGE. Are there?

JULIANA. Small things, yes; dozens of them.

GEORGE. *(Now totally confused.)* What do you mean it's a relief?

JULIANA. For lovely Aunt Rena, Georgie!

GEORGE. Ah. Yes.

HEDDA. *(Covering.)* You'll miss her terribly, Miss Tesman.

JULIANA. We all will. But we must rise above. Immediately after the funeral the first thing I'm going to do is get somebody for her little room. Somebody about her age; bedridden, too. There'll be plenty of applicants, I'm sure.

HEDDA. You're going to take on that burden again — and a total stranger?

JULIANA. That's not a burden, Hedda. I need someone to live for. Thinking only of yourself and your problems can be very boring and very unhealthy. And please God there'll soon be work in this house that an old aunt can lend a hand with.

HEDDA. *(Quickly.)* We've got to talk about that Berna creature.

GEORGE. Bertha? What about Bertha?

HEDDA. She's becoming intolerable.

JULIANA. I'm sure she's not herself today, Hedda. She devoted her entire life to Auntie Rena. Try to be patient with her for the time being, will you? I'll speak to her later. *(As she leaves.)* Such a peculiar thought came into my head as I was coming here tonight. I thought: Rena is still here with us in her own little room; but she's also with your father, dear Joachim. Isn't that strange?

GEORGE. *(Flatly.)* Amazing, Auntie Juju, yes.

JULIANA. She'll be telling him about your doctorate and all the ins and outs of the professorship. And most important of all, Hedda — your good news! I'll see myself out. Let Bertha get over these difficult days. I'll have a word with her then. *(She exits.)*

GEORGE. Your good news, she said?

HEDDA. Oh shut up! What's the matter with you today?

GEORGE. It's Eilert, Hedda. Can't get him out of my head. I'm so worried about him. I'm afraid he might do himself an injury.

HEDDA. Why do you say that?

GEORGE. Well, I dropped into his lodgings just to reassure him that the manuscript was safe here. But he wasn't there. Then I bumped into Thea down at the harbour. She seemed to be very distressed. She told me Eilert had been here this morning.

HEDDA. Just after you left.

GEORGE. And that he announced he'd torn the manuscript into pieces. He didn't say that, did he?

HEDDA. He did.

GEORGE. He must be demented. Why wouldn't he be? But you told him we have it?

HEDDA. No.

GEORGE. You didn't?!

HEDDA. Did you tell Thea?

GEORGE. You should have told him, Hedda. The poor creature might do something desperate.

HEDDA. Did you tell Thea?

GEORGE. No. Give me the envelope. I'll try his lodgings again.

HEDDA. The envelope is gone.

GEORGE. Gone where?

HEDDA. I burned it.

GEORGE. Eilert's manuscript?

HEDDA. In the stove.

GEORGE. Oh God, no, Hedda!

HEDDA. The maid'll hear you.

GEORGE. You burned Loevborg's amazing manuscript?

HEDDA. I did.

GEORGE. But that's a criminal act, Hedda. An immoral act, too. My gentle Hedda couldn't do something as immoral as that, could she?

HEDDA. Listen to me. You came home from the judge's party this morning; and you told me Eilert had read to you alone for a full hour in the judge's breakfast room; and you said you thought it was the most amazing book you'd ever read; and you said you suddenly knew you were jealous of Eilert Loevborg because you felt it was very unfair that this weak and damaged man should be given that great talent —

GEORGE. I know — I know — I know I said all that. But if I said I was jealous I didn't for a second mean that —

HEDDA. So I burned the manuscript because I couldn't allow anyone to overshadow you.

GEORGE. You burned the — ?

HEDDA. I did it for you, George.

GEORGE. For me?

HEDDA. How could that be an immoral act?

GEORGE. Oh my God ...

HEDDA. I did it for you, George. Believe me. For my husband. *(Long pause.)*

GEORGE. *(Almost whispers, in awe.)* That you love me so profoundly, Hedda, I never knew that ... never ever ... no idea ... none whatever ... What an astonishing, what a humbling revelation ... For my sake ... My goodness what can I say? ... Oh my goodness, I'm speechless, love ...

HEDDA. *(Recklessly, wildly.)* And now to fill your cup to overflowing. In four months' time — all being well, as the quaint expression has it — all being well I'm going to have a — No, no, no, no, no. Tell you what. I'll get prescient Auntie Juju to spell it out for you. She has known almost as long as I have. *(Pause.)*

GEORGE. In four months time you're going to have — ? You're

not serious, Hedda!

HEDDA. Yes.

GEORGE. You really believe that in four months time — all being well — ? You really are serious, aren't you?

HEDDA. Deadly.

GEORGE. Wishful thinking. Trust me. That's what that is. You're so eager, so desperately keen, your judgment is clouded and you've convinced yourself it really is happening. But it's not, Hedda my love. Believe me. Be sensible, darling — just isn't true. *(Brief pause. He gazes at her.)* Yes, it is! It is, isn't it? Oh my God, yes, it's true. You know very well, don't you? Yes, it is true! I mean, women have this amazing intuitive sense about all kinds of things and they're so often accurate, aren't they? Oh yes, yes, yes, you know for certain — not a second of doubt — that in four months — all being very, very well — you're going to have a —

HEDDA. *(Bitterly.)* For God's sake, man! *(Pause. George is stunned. He drops on to a chair.)*

GEORGE. Oh, Hedda, my illustrious queen, this must be the happiest moment of my entire … *(Pause. Silence. Then the three things — that she burned the manuscript, that she burned the manuscript for him, that she is pregnant — all three collide in his head and detonate. Now he is suddenly released — propelled — hurled into exaggerated, manic activity. He takes her hand, kisses it a dozen times, strokes his face with it and then returns it formally to her lap. He drops on his knees and salaams before her. He grabs a bundle of flowers and presents them to her. He takes several blooms and wreaths his head with them. He runs up to the back room, plays a few seconds of "Chopsticks," runs back to the drawing room. He runs — dances — round the table, beating out a tattoo on it with his hands. During all this extravaganza Hedda sits absolutely still, rigid, upright, her eyes closed tight, her face a mask. Throughout his buffoonery George pours out this commentary at top speed:)* It will be a boy — and such a handsome boy he'll be! Congratulations, Hedda darling! We'll call him George the Second. No, we won't. We'll call him Joachim after his grandfather. Handsome Joachim the Second. Do you agree? Great! But it may be a girl. And what an exquisite girl she'll be! Congratulations, Hedda darling! And we'll call her Hedda, won't we? Another celestial Hedda Tesman that will make this world even more numinous. No! Can't be Hedda! There can be only one Hedda, the unique Hedda who loves her husband inordinately. Juliana, then. No, no, no, not Juliana.

Rena! Yes, exquisite Rena Tesman! Yes, that's a brilliant decision. Well done, Hedda! And we'll not make the announcement until after the funeral. We'll tell Auntie Juju first and then we'll tell Bertha. Bertha will be so delighted. Hold on — what about Bertha for a name! Now that's a thought! Wouldn't she be thrilled! No, no; don't jump about; stop changing your mind. Stick with Rena. Although it would give Bertha such a lift! Bertha Tesman! No. Maybe not this time. Next time maybe. And we'll have to tell Thea Elvsted, dedicated-to-her-anxieties Thea. I know you have reservations about her, Hedda. But she's a very good-hearted woman and I know she will rejoice with us. And Judge Brack of course. "What splendid news, Tesman! As the Americans have it — gee-whiz." And what about Eilert Loevborg? No, we'll not tell Eilert; not yet anyway. I don't know why but some-how it doesn't seem appropriate to tell Eilert. And which room will be the nursery? I'll leave that decision to you. And I'll use the other room for my library. And riding lessons! Put their names down immediately. They're bound to be natural horse-people like their mother and their grandfather, the general. The piano lessons! You wouldn't want to take on that job. No, no, much too boring. I'm told a young teacher has just set up shop two doors down from the Planetarium. They say she's very enthusiastic. I'll have a word with her next week. They'll be superb pianists! My goodness … oh my goodness … (*He suddenly collapses on to the couch. He covers his face with his hands and lies there perfectly still and silent for five seconds.*)

HEDDA. (*Still rigid, eyes closed tight, body erect.*) Oh God … dear God … oh dear God … (*Suddenly George is galvanized again. He leaps to his feet and resumes his buffoonery.*)

GEORGE. And slippers, Hedda! Slippers, slippers, embroidered slippers! On their very first birthday and on every birthday after-wards I'll embroider a wildflower on their slippers, Joachim's and Rena's. I can't embroider — but I'll learn. Isn't that a good idea? Traditions must be maintained. (*He is suddenly calm and quiet again and speaks softly and slowly.*) Oh yes, oh yes, absolutely … this must be the happiest moment of my entire —

HEDDA. (*As before.*) Will you tell Auntie Juju?

GEORGE. She'll be the very first to know.

HEDDA. That I burned Eilert's book? (*She now opens her eyes and gazes at George.*)

GEORGE. No, no, not that. She must never know that, Hedda. But what I would very much like her to know is that you did it for my sake. Maybe being pregnant, Hedda darling, perhaps that's what gave you the determination, did it? Or perhaps all young brides are as audacious on their husband's behalf as you?

HEDDA. Ask your auntie that, too. Won't she know?

GEORGE. *(Laughs uneasily.)* I don't think she would, Hedda. She's a single girl after all ... *(Suddenly miserable.)* All the same, Eilert's manuscript — terrible, just terrible. That is a real catastrophe. Can't even begin to think about that. *(Thea, very agitated, rushes in from the hall.)*

HEDDA. Thea!

THEA. I'm sorry — I'm back — forgive me.

HEDDA. What's wrong, Thea?

GEORGE. It's Eilert!

THEA. Something has happened to him, Hedda.

GEORGE. *(To Hedda.)*. I told you, didn't I?

HEDDA. Stop fidgeting. What has happened?

THEA. I don't know. An accident of some sort, I think. When I got back to my lodgings, they were whispering about him. Nobody seemed to know anything for sure. There were rumours of all sorts about what happened last night.

GEORGE. That's all they are — rumours. I was with him last night. He went straight home to bed.

HEDDA. What rumours?

THEA. Something about a brawl — and the police being called — and a gun being fired. He's in the hospital, it seems.

HEDDA. Nonsense.

GEORGE. Oh my God ...

THEA. I went to his lodging to find out what I could, but they wouldn't even speak to me there.

GEORGE. I'm going to the police — to the hospital. Eilert's in serious trouble. I told you that, Hedda, didn't I?

HEDDA. You're going nowhere.

GEORGE. I have got to —

HEDDA. Keep out of this. This has nothing to do with you, nothing at all. *(Judge Brack enters, looking very serious.)*

GEORGE. Judge Brack!

BRACK. I had to see you. *(To George.)* My condolences on your aunt, Tesman.

GEORGE. Thank you.

BRACK. *(To Hedda.)* And to you, madam. *(Hedda bows.)* She was a gentle lady. I'll call on Miss Juliana later.

GEORGE. Take a seat, Judge.

BRACK. I'm here about another matter altogether.

THEA. Eilert!

BRACK. You know already, Mrs. Elvsted?

THEA. I've heard rumours, that's all.

BRACK. Yes, it's Loevborg.

GEORGE. *(To Hedda.)* See? *(To Brack.)* For God's sake, tell us! *(Brack shrugs.)*

BRACK. Loevborg has been taken to hospital. He doesn't have long.

THEA. Oh God, no — oh God ...

HEDDA. So soon?

THEA. *(Beginning to cry.)* And we parted in anger when I saw him last, Hedda.

HEDDA. Quiet.

THEA. I must go to him. I've got to see him before he dies.

BRACK. No point, Mrs. Elvsted. They aren't allowing any visitors.

THEA. Tell me what happened.

GEORGE. But he — I mean — he didn't do it to himself, did he?

HEDDA. Of course he did.

GEORGE. Hedda!

BRACK. Mrs. Tesman's assumption is correct.

THEA. Oh my God ...

GEORGE. Suicide then?

HEDDA. Shot himself.

BRACK. Correct.

GEORGE. Good God!

BRACK. This afternoon. Between three and four, they think.

GEORGE. In his lodging?

BRACK. *(Momentarily confused.)* In his lodging? — yes — I imagine yes —

THEA. That can't be right. I saw him later than four.

BRACK. Whenever then. I haven't got the details. All I know is that he shot himself in the chest.

THEA. Eilert Loevborg shouldn't have died like that. Dear, dear God ...

HEDDA. *(To Brack.)* In the chest?

BRACK. According to the police.

HEDDA. Not in the temple?

BRACK. I was told the chest.

HEDDA. The heart. Not inappropriate.

BRACK. What do you mean? *(Hedda turns away.)*

GEORGE. And it's a bad wound?

BRACK. He may be dead already.

THEA. The judge is right. I know in my heart it's all over. Oh Hedda, Hedda …

HEDDA. How do you know all this?

BRACK. The police told me.

HEDDA. Thank heaven — at last something accomplished consciously.

GEORGE. What do you mean?

HEDDA. And achieved with beauty.

GEORGE. For God's sake Hedda!

THEA. What's beautiful about it?

HEDDA. He settled his account with life after a lot of consideration and with a lot of fortitude.

THEA. I don't understand what she's saying.

HEDDA. And he settled with the style I expected from Eilert Loevborg. Yes, all that was appropriate; all that has a beauty.

THEA. Rubbish. He shot himself because he was a weak creature and because he was in despair.

GEORGE. Thea's right. I remember, even as a student, he used to have terrible stretches of depression.

THEA. Don't I know my Eilert? Some dark impulse took possession of him, just as he must have been possessed when he tore up our manuscript.

GEORGE. Thea's right.

HEDDA. I know Thea's wrong.

BRACK. Tearing up the manuscript — when did that happen?

THEA. Last night.

BRACK. Remarkable.

GEORGE. I just can't believe that the brilliant Eilert Loevborg would end it all like this and not make sure that the "authentic thing," the "genuine article" that would have immortalised him — that that was all secure. He knew it was his succès d'estime.

THEA. If only it could be pieced together again.

GEORGE. I'd give anything in the world for that.

THEA. It might be possible. What do you think?

GEORGE. I don't see how.

THEA. I think it just might. I kept all the notes he used to dictate from. I took them with me when I left home. *(She searches through her bag and produces sheets of paper.)* There. You're right — it's hopeless. *(She hands the papers to George.)*

GEORGE. You kept them all?

THEA. They're a mess, I'm afraid.

GEORGE. Maybe if they could be put in some sort of order … You know exactly what there is here?

THEA. What do you think?

GEORGE. Maybe …

THEA. All I know is that nothing's missing.

GEORGE. Maybe we can, Thea. Yes, I believe maybe we can.

THEA. Do you?

GEORGE. Yes, yes, yes, for Eilert's sake. We'll do it for him. I'll give over a year to it — two if I have to. For Eilert's sake.

HEDDA. A very moral decision, George.

GEORGE. He was my friend.

HEDDA. Ah.

GEORGE. If it's to be done, it must be done in an organised fashion. There must be nothing sentimental about it.

THEA. You're so right.

GEORGE. Let's first see what we have. Where will we sit? Let's go into the back room. Will you excuse us?

THEA. I think we can do it, Hedda. I know we can.

HEDDA. Good for you, little Miss Rysing. *(George and Thea go up to the back room. They sit at the table with their backs to Hedda and Brack. They begin sorting out the papers.)* There's such a sense of release in what Loevborg has done.

BRACK. He must have thought so.

HEDDA. I'm talking about *me!* The satisfaction in knowing that a destiny *can* be moulded; that you *can* nudge a man to achieve something daring and beautiful.

BRACK. *(Smiling.)* Influencing destinies is far beyond my modest ambitions.

HEDDA. *(Sharply.)* You don't have to proclaim that, Judge. At heart you're just a commonplace bourgeois. Even your precious affectations can't disguise that.

BRACK. And the bourgeois in me suspects Eilert Loevborg meant more to you than you like to admit. Am I right?

HEDDA. I'm not in the stand. I've said all I'm going to say about Eilert Loevborg's final accomplishment. It had symmetry. It had grace.

It was triumph. Yes, Judge Brack, that destiny was important to me.

BRACK. And for that reason I'm hesitant to shatter your illusions, dear Hedda. The record of events I adduced was incomplete — for Mrs. Elvsted's sake. He was still alive when they rushed him to the hospital. He died within an hour. He never regained consciousness. And he didn't shoot himself in his lodging.

HEDDA. *(Impatiently.)* So — so — so?

BRACK. And it wasn't "achieved" deliberately. Almost certainly an accident.

HEDDA. Nonsense.

BRACK. And in the boudoir of the cruelty-to-animals lady — what's her name? — the closet classicist — the artillery expert —

HEDDA. *(Impatiently.)* Where? — where? — who? —

BRACK. Mademoiselle Circe!

HEDDA. That's a lie! In her bedroom?

BRACK. Where he spent the entire afternoon. Drunk of course. He had gone back there to fetch something he claims she had taken from him.

HEDDA. How drunk?

BRACK. Blotto. Talked a lot of gibberish about a lost child. I supposed he meant his manuscript but Mrs. Elvsted tells me he destroyed that himself. Perhaps his wallet then. Anyhow that's where he was found; in Circe's bedroom; with a discharged pistol in his breast pocket; blood pumping from a wound where he was — as they say … plugged.

HEDDA. But in the heart?

BRACK. Not the heart. *(He points to his groin.)*

HEDDA. Oh God…!

BRACK. And one further disagreeable detail: the police suspect the pistol was stolen.

HEDDA. Another lie! He didn't steal it! I —

BRACK. *(Rapidly, softly.)* Don't be so stupid, Hedda. It must have been stolen. The other explanation is … unthinkable. *(George and Thea come down from the other room. Their hands are filled with papers.)*

GEORGE. The light up there is poor and we need more space to spread the stuff out. May we use your desk, too?

HEDDA. By all means. Hold on — let me tidy it.

GEORGE. It's fine.

HEDDA. I said I'll tidy it. You don't need this stuff. *(She takes the revolver case from the drawer, covers it with sheets of music and goes up to the back room and off to the left — taking the revolver case with her. George and Thea begin working at the table. They also use the desk for filing.)*

GEORGE. *(To Thea.)* The first thing we must do is try to establish the date of each of these pages. Otherwise we'll never get them into sequence.

THEA. I don't think they're all dated.

GEORGE. What's that?

THEA. April seventh.

GEORGE. And that?

THEA. July nineteenth.

GEORGE. It *is* a mess. *(Hedda returns. She stands behind Thea and runs her fingers through her hair.)*

HEDDA. And how is the Loevborg memorial coming along?

THEA. *(Unhappily.)* Hard to say, Hedda. The stuff's in chaos.

HEDDA. I have no doubt you're the woman to impose order on it — in your own diffident way.

GEORGE. It isn't going to be easy but I believe we'll pull something together. As you know, Hedda, I'm first-rate at cataloguing documents. *(Hedda sits on the footstool. Brack stands behind her. They speak softly.)*

HEDDA. And the police think the pistol was stolen?

BRACK. Softly if you would. Let's assume he stole it from here. He was here this morning, was he not? There are witnesses — not least the redoubtable Bertha. Then you and he were alone here together; and at some point, perhaps, you left him by himself for a few minutes — perhaps you went looking for Bertha or perhaps there was somebody at the door. Anyhow he was left by himself. Where were the pistols?

HEDDA. Locked in that — *(She breaks off suddenly. They exchange looks.)*

BRACK. They weren't locked, were they?

HEDDA. You're right. They were lying on the table.

BRACK. Much more likely. And have you looked to see if both pistols are still there? Why trouble? I saw the pistol in the police station and I recognised it from yesterday — *(He mimes.)* — "Bang-bang. It's only a game" — that one. Anyhow the police have that gun now and are endeavouring to trace the owner.

HEDDA. Will they succeed?

BRACK. *(Leaning down to her ear and whispering.)* Not as long as

I keep mum.

HEDDA. Will you?

BRACK. At keeping mum I'm masterly. In fact I can't recall ever being a … snitch. Is that the noun?

HEDDA. And if you don't keep mum?

BRACK. You could always tell them he stole it.

HEDDA. I'd rather die.

BRACK. *(Smiling.)* People say that, beautiful Hedda. It is estimable and they mean it. But they never do it.

HEDDA. And if they should trace the owner?

BRACK. Oh, then there'd be an enormous scandal — the type of scandal you have such a horror of. A court case, of course — you and classical Circe playing leading roles. She will tell us all how it happened. Was it an accident or was it manslaughter? Perhaps he was threatening her? Did the pistol go off as he pulled it from his jacket? Or did Miss Circe pull the pistol from him, shoot him and return the gun to his pocket? That would be in character. And as the case progresses, Mrs. Tesman, you're certain to be asked the key question: did you give him the pistol? And if it were to emerge that you did give it to him, what conclusions will people draw from that? But of course you're in no danger whatever as long as I don't snitch — may I employ the word as a verb?

HEDDA. I'm altogether in your power then?

BRACK. Hedda, darling —

HEDDA. Forever?

BRACK. You don't think for a second I'd abuse that position?

HEDDA. But you'd own me! *(She jumps up.)* No, Judge, no! That won't happen!

BRACK. People can learn to live with what they can't change, Hedda Tesman.

HEDDA. Hedda Gabler can't, Judge Brack. *(She goes to the table where George and Thea are working. Forces cheeriness:)* I have a sense things are going very well here.

GEORGE. Too early to say. All I know is it's going to be an enormous task — *if* we can do it.

HEDDA. It must feel a little strange for you, Thea, working beside George the way you did with Eilert Loevborg.

THEA. I suppose it is — yes.

HEDDA. But a new collaborator — there's an excitement in that, surely?

THEA. A great excitement. Imagine if I could inspire him too.

HEDDA. I believe you will. Give it time, Thea. Then step by step. Remember?

GEORGE. You're being facetious, darling, but I am aware of a ... something in the atmosphere.

HEDDA. *(To Thea.)* There!

GEORGE. I am — really!

HEDDA. It's called inspiration, George. Don't funk the word. Is funk acceptable, Judge?

BRACK. Perfectly. And interestingly, of English origin, not American.

GEORGE. Inspiration or whatever, you're interrupting it. Off you go and chat to the judge.

BRACK. Oxford slang actually. Eighteenth-century.

HEDDA. So I'm of no use to you two soul-mates?

GEORGE. Will you please entertain my wife for me, Judge Brack?

BRACK. Nothing would pleasure me more.

HEDDA. I'm suddenly very tired. Would you mind if I lay down on the sofa for a while?

BRACK. Not in the least.

HEDDA. Just a short nap. *(She goes up to the back room and pulls the curtains behind her.)*

GEORGE. *(To Thea.)* I can't read his handwriting. There's a date scribbled there — what is it?

THEA. Either October the sixth or the eighth. It's the sixth. *(Suddenly Hedda begins playing a wild, near-manic dance on the piano.)*

THEA. What's — ?

GEORGE. *(Leaping to his feet.)* Please, Hedda, darling! For heaven's sake! Not tonight! Think of Auntie Rena! And Eilert! Please! *(The music stops. George sits down again. Hedda puts her head out through the curtains.)*

HEDDA. You're so right ... thoughtless ... forgive me ... so from now on ... *(She puts her index finger to her lips and utters a "shhh-hh" that goes on for a very, very long time. She withdraws again, closing the curtain behind her.)*

GEORGE. She *is* tired. And very upset. And then us sitting here and working with Eilert's material, maybe that's a little insensitive, is it?

THEA. We're all tired. It has been a long day.

GEORGE. There's a thought, Thea. You could move in with Auntie Juju — Rena's room is empty now; and I could join you there every evening. We could work in peace there and we wouldn't annoy anybody.

THEA. Would Miss Juliana agree?

HEDDA. *(Offstage.)* I hear every word you're saying. What will I do alone here every evening?

GEORGE. Could the judge be coaxed into keeping you company?

BRACK. *(To George.)* You make it sound like a chore. *(To Hedda.)* It would be a most special delectation.

HEDDA. *(Offstage.)* Yes, you'd love that, Judge, wouldn't you? The only rooster in the yard.

BRACK. *(Musing to himself.)* The only rooster in the yard ... The only bull in the pen ... The only cock on the dunghill ... Why does it have to be so farmyard? Why not the only orchid in the conservatory? The only butterfly in the wheatfield? The only lark in the prairie? *(A sudden shot offstage. All leap to their feet.)*

GEORGE. She's playing with those damned pistols again! For God's sake, Hedda! ... *(Bertha rushes in.)*

BERTHA. Did I hear a — ? *(George flings the curtains back and rushes into the back room. Thea follows him. Hedda has shot herself in the head. She is lying on the sofa. There is blood everywhere.)*

GEORGE. Hedda! Oh Jesus Christ...! Oh Hedda! Jesus Christ!

THEA. Oh my God!

BERTHA. No, no, no — please — please — no, no.

GEORGE. *(In total shock.)* She has shot herself in the temple, Judge Brack.

BRACK. *(Refusing to hear.)* Can't hear what the man's saying.

THEA. Oh my God, George ...

BRACK. What are you saying, Tesman?

GEORGE. She has shot herself in the temple, Judge Brack.

BRACK. That's a damned lie!

BERTHA. God forgive the poor unhappy creature.

THEA. George ... George ...

BERTHA. May God in his mercy overlook all her human faults.

GEORGE. She has killed herself, Judge Brack, and handsome young Joachim or maybe exquisite young Rena, Judge Brack.

BRACK. Never! I will not have that!

GEORGE. In the temple, Judge Brack.

BRACK. That's a damned lie! For God's sake, reasonable people just don't do things like that. *(Fade to black.)*

End of Play

PROPERTY LIST

Hat, parasol
Blood
Flowers and vase
lip plaster
Empty suitcase
Curtains
Package wrapped in paper
Old piano
Slippers embroidered with flowers
Card
Envelope
Writing table
Bookcase
Pistol
Manuscript
Cigars
Photo album
Tray, glasses, canapés
Lamp
Letter
Hand mirror
Sheet music
Wood-burning stove
Black ribbons in a cap

SOUND EFFECTS

Manic piano music
Rapid chords on the piano